# THE NATION REUNITED
## War's Aftermath

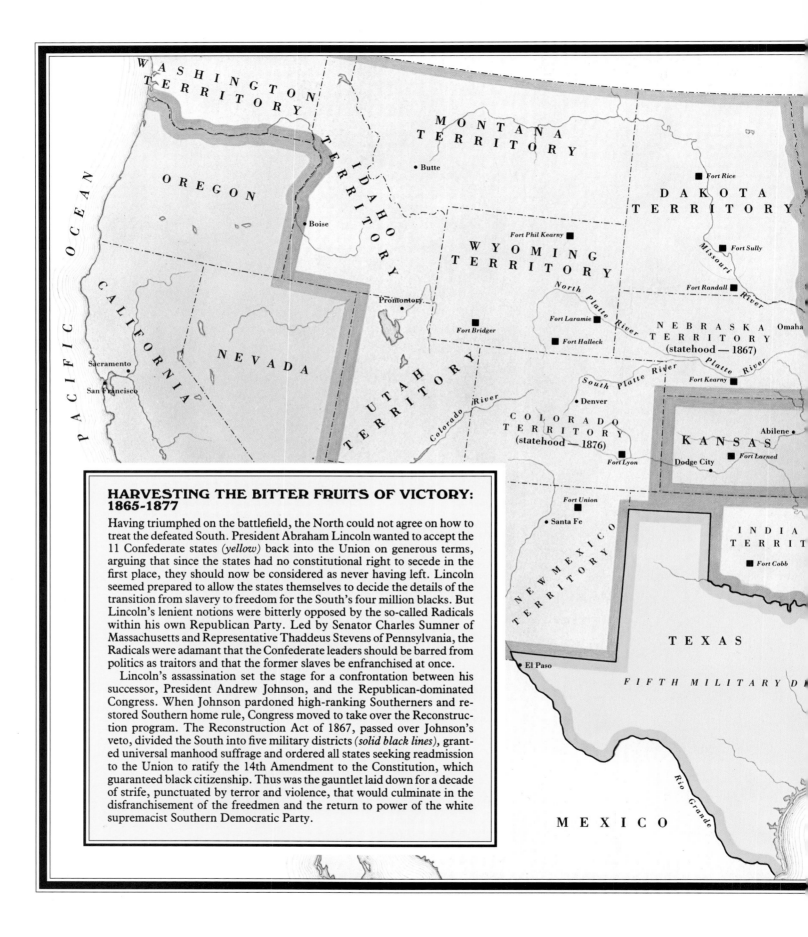

## HARVESTING THE BITTER FRUITS OF VICTORY: 1865-1877

Having triumphed on the battlefield, the North could not agree on how to treat the defeated South. President Abraham Lincoln wanted to accept the 11 Confederate states *(yellow)* back into the Union on generous terms, arguing that since the states had no constitutional right to secede in the first place, they should now be considered as never having left. Lincoln seemed prepared to allow the states themselves to decide the details of the transition from slavery to freedom for the South's four million blacks. But Lincoln's lenient notions were bitterly opposed by the so-called Radicals within his own Republican Party. Led by Senator Charles Sumner of Massachusetts and Representative Thaddeus Stevens of Pennsylvania, the Radicals were adamant that the Confederate leaders should be barred from politics as traitors and that the former slaves be enfranchised at once.

Lincoln's assassination set the stage for a confrontation between his successor, President Andrew Johnson, and the Republican-dominated Congress. When Johnson pardoned high-ranking Southerners and restored Southern home rule, Congress moved to take over the Reconstruction program. The Reconstruction Act of 1867, passed over Johnson's veto, divided the South into five military districts *(solid black lines)*, granted universal manhood suffrage and ordered all states seeking readmission to the Union to ratify the 14th Amendment to the Constitution, which guaranteed black citizenship. Thus was the gauntlet laid down for a decade of strife, punctuated by terror and violence, that would culminate in the disfranchisement of the freedmen and the return to power of the white supremacist Southern Democratic Party.

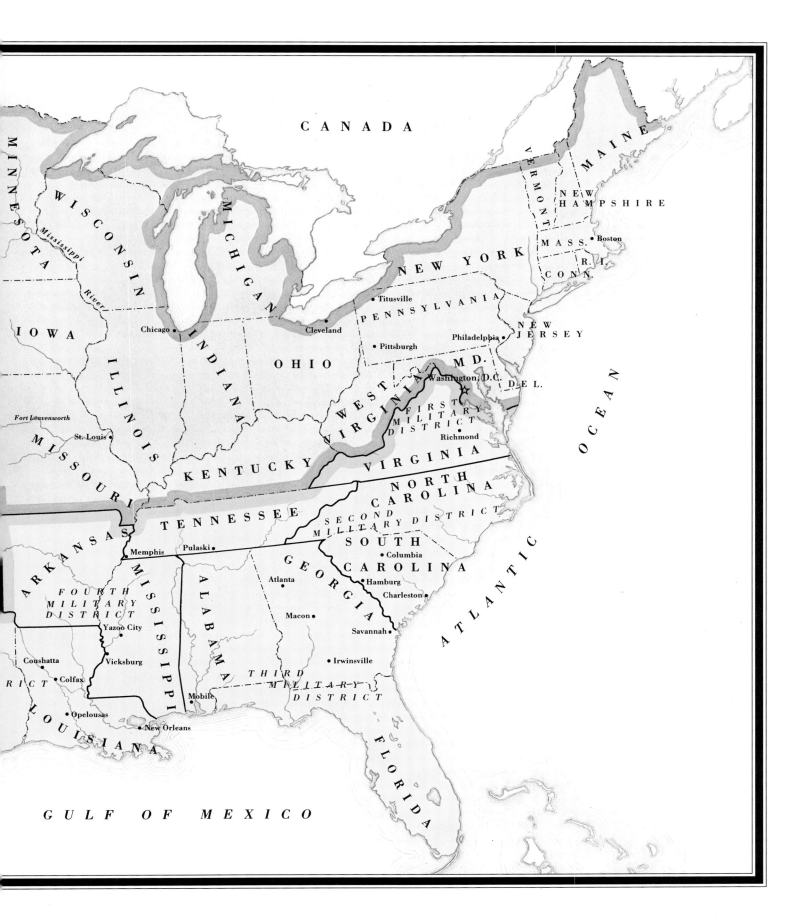

This volume is one of a series that chronicles in full
the events of the American Civil War, 1861-1865.

*The Cover:* In July of 1913, a pair of old soldiers — one
in gray, the other in blue — join hands at the 50th anniversary of the Battle of Gettysburg. For most veterans, service in the Civil War had been the high point of
their lives: "If there is any part of your life in which
you were where you should have been, and did what
you should have done," a former officer told a group of
aging comrades, "it is the great Olympiad of '61 to '65.
What have you felt or looked on since that is not piti-
fully small in comparison?"

For information on and a full description of any of the
Time-Life Books series listed on this page, please call
1-800-621-7026 or write:
Reader Information
Time-Life Customer Service
P.O. Box C-32068
Richmond, Virginia 23261-2068

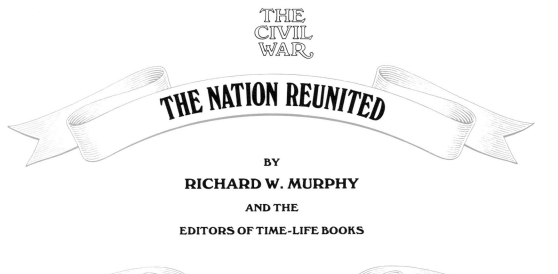

# THE CIVIL WAR

# THE NATION REUNITED

BY

## RICHARD W. MURPHY

AND THE

### EDITORS OF TIME-LIFE BOOKS

### War's Aftermath

TIME-LIFE BOOKS, ALEXANDRIA, VIRGINIA

## TIME-LIFE BOOKS

EDITOR-IN-CHIEF: Thomas H. Flaherty

*Director of Editorial Resources:* Elise D. Ritter-Clough
*Executive Art Director:* Ellen Robling
*Director of Photography and Research:*
John Conrad Weiser
*Editorial Board:* Dale M. Brown, Janet Cave, Roberta
Conlan, Robert Doyle, Laura Foreman, Jim Hicks,
Rita Thievon Mullin, Henry Woodhead
*Assistant Director of Editorial Resources:* Norma E. Shaw

PRESIDENT: John D. Hall

*Vice President and Director of Marketing:*
Nancy K. Jones
*Editorial Director:* Russell B. Adams, Jr.
*Director of Production Services:* Robert N. Carr
*Production Manager:* Prudence G. Harris
*Supervisor of Quality Control:* James King

Editorial Operations
*Production:* Celia Beattie
*Library:* Louise D. Forstall
*Computer Composition:* Deborah G. Tait (Manager),
Monika D. Thayer, Janet Barnes Syring,
Lillian Daniels
*Interactive Media Specialist:* Patti H. Cass

Time-Life Books is a division of Time Life
Incorporated

PRESIDENT AND CEO: John M. Fahey, Jr.

**The Civil War**
Series Director: Thomas H. Flaherty
*Designer:* Edward Frank
*Series Administrators:* Jane Edwin, Judith W. Shanks

Editorial Staff for *Nation Reunited*
*Associate Editor:* Kristin Baker (pictures)
*Staff Writers:* Janet Cave, Margery A. duMond, John
Newton, Brian C. Pohanka
*Researchers:* Stephanie Lewis, Trudy Pearson
(principals); Karen F. Monks, Gwen Mullen
*Assistant Designers:* William Alan Pitts,
Lorraine D. Rivard
*Copy Coordinators:* Vivian Noble, Ruth Baja Williams
*Picture Coordinator:* Betty H. Weatherley
*Editorial Assistant:* Donna Fountain
*Special Contributors:* Thomas A. Lewis (text),
Brian E. McGinn

Correspondents: Elisabeth Kraemer-Singh (Bonn);
Maria Vincenza Aloisi (Paris); Ann Natanson (Rome).
Valuable assistance was also provided by: Vanessa
Kramer (London); Liz Brown, Christina Lieberman
(New York).

*The Author:*
Richard W. Murphy is a former *Time* editor now living in
Paris. He is the author of two previous Time-Life Books:
*Status and Conformity* in the Human Behavior series and
*The World of Cézanne* in the Library of Art. He served
as a staff writer and editor on the Time-Life Books World
War II series and the Civil War series.

*The Consultants:*
Colonel John R. Elting, USA (Ret.), a former Associate
Professor at West Point, is the author of *Battles for Scandinavia* in the Time-Life Books World War II series and of
*The Battle of Bunker's Hill, The Battles of Saratoga, Mili-
tary History and Atlas of the Napoleonic Wars, American
Army Life* and *The Superstrategists.* Co-author of *A Dic-
tionary of Soldier Talk,* he is also editor of the three vol-
umes of *Military Uniforms in America, 1755-1867,* and associate editor of *The West Point Atlas of American Wars.*

William A. Frassanito, a Civil War historian and lecturer
specializing in photograph analysis, is the author of two
award-winning studies, *Gettysburg: A Journey in Time* and
*Antietam: The Photographic Legacy of America's Bloodiest
Day,* and a companion volume, *Grant and Lee, The Virginia Campaigns.* He has also served as chief consultant to the
photographic history series *The Image of War.*

Les Jensen, Director of the Second Armored Division
Museum, Fort Hood, Texas, specializes in Civil War arti-
facts and is a conservator of historic flags. He is a contribu-
tor to *The Image of War* series, consultant for numerous
Civil War publications and museums, and a member of
the Company of Military Historians. He was formerly Curator of the U.S. Army Transportation Museum at Fort
Eustis, Virginia, and before that Curator of the Museum
of the Confederacy in Richmond, Virginia.

Michael McAfee specializes in military uniforms and has
been Curator of Uniforms and History at the West Point
Museum since 1970. A fellow of the Company of Military
Historians, he coedited with Colonel Elting *Long Endure:
The Civil War Years,* and he collaborated with Frederick
Todd on *American Military Equipage.* He is the author of
*Artillery of the American Revolution, 1775-1783,* and has
written numerous articles for *Military Images Magazine.*

James P. Shenton, Professor of History at Columbia University, is a specialist in 19th-century American political
and social history, with particular emphasis on the Civil
War period. He is the author of *Robert John Walker* and
*Reconstruction South.*

Library of Congress Cataloguing in Publication Data
Murphy, Richard W.
 The Nation reunited.
 (The Civil War)
 Bibliography: p.
 Includes index.
 1. Reconstruction. 2. United States — Politics and
government — 1865-1877. I. Time-Life Books.
II. Title. III. Series.
E668.M93 1987    973.8'1    87-9917
ISBN 0-8094-4792-4
ISBN 0-8094-4793-2 (lib. bdg.)

# CONTENTS

# An Unforgettable Last Hurrah

For the proud soldiers of the North, one final mission remained in the spring of 1865 before they were mustered out of service and scattered to their distant homes. At the urging of Secretary of War Edwin Stanton, President Andrew Johnson ordered the Union armies to stage a grand review through the heart of Washington, D.C.

It required two full days for the estimated 150,000 troops to march past the cheering crowds that thronged Pennsylvania Avenue. On May 23, Major General George G. Meade's Army of the Potomac paraded through the capital with a precision that moved one observer to call them "the greatest army that ever went to war." Schoolchildren serenaded the marchers with patriotic songs and strewed their route with flowers.

The rough appearance of Major General William T. Sherman's Army of Georgia and Army of Tennessee as they strode up the avenue the next day contrasted sharply with that of Meade's more polished soldiers. Sherman's "bummers" provided a touch of comic relief: Some rode mules while others dangled chickens and cured hams from their muskets. They were joined by dogs, goats, raccoons and even a monkey.

For the men in the ranks, the review was an experience never to be forgotten. "The very air seemed freighted with gladness," one private recalled. "I felt that the pleasures of that day fully repaid me for all the hardships, privations, dangers and suffering that I had endured during all those years of strife and carnage."

**A detail from the Veteran Reserve Corps guards the elaborate presidential reviewing stand on Pennsylvania Avenue, near the White House. Among the dignitaries who can be seen on the platform are President Johnson, Secretary of the Navy Gideon Welles and Generals Meade, Sherman and Ulysses S. Grant.**

A regiment of Union infantry in column of companies marches past Willard's Hotel. "The glittering muskets looked like a solid mass of steel," General Sherman observed, "moving with the regularity of a pendulum."

Major General Francis Preston Blair, mounted on a white horse, doffs his hat as he rides at the head of XVII Corps during the review of Sherman's army. As he passed the reviewing stand, Blair, like the other corps commanders, saluted with his sword, then dismounted and joined the dignitaries seated with President Johnson.

Mounted artillery officers of the Army of the Potomac precede columns of guns and caissons moving up Pennsylvania Avenue. As a safety precaution, all ammunition was removed from the limbers and caissons before the parade began.

Each brigade taking part in the review was followed by six horse-drawn ambulances *(foreground)*. A soldier in the 150th New York wrote that "the rumbling of their wheels seemed like a vast, ghostly procession of the great host of suffering ones who had ridden in them."

Spectators gather at the Capitol (*inset*) to witness the beginning of the Grand Review. The building was draped with black crepe in memory of fallen Union soldiers, and in mourning for Abraham Lincoln.

Expectant onlookers fill the bleachers erected near the U.S. Treasury building. "The crowd was hushed," one newspaper reported, "and waited as if for the grand dénouement of a great play."

Major General Romeyn Ayres's division of V Corps pauses at Market Square to adjust its alignment before continuing up Pennsylvania Avenue to the White House. Ayres's leading brigade was composed of regiments clad in colorful Zouave attire.

# The North Divided

*"The war feeling here is like a burning bush with a wet blanket wrapped around it. Looked at from the outside, the fire seems quenched. But just peep under the blanket and there it is, all alive, and eating, eating in."*

JOHN TROWBRIDGE, NORTHERN CORRESPONDENT TOURING THE SOUTH IN 1866

1

Senator Benjamin F. Wade of Ohio, long a fervent enemy of slavery and the Confederacy, strode into Suite 68 of Kirkwood House in Washington, D.C., on the sad evening of April 15, 1865, and grasped Andrew Johnson by the hand. A gathering in Johnson's quarters, held to celebrate his elevation to the presidency of the United States, was muted by grief and shock: Only that morning Abraham Lincoln had been pronounced dead of an assassin's bullet.

But Wade, who sometimes kept a rifle in his desk, had no time for sorrow or for the past; it was the future that concerned him. "Mr. Johnson, I thank God that you are here," he said. "Lincoln had too much of the milk of human kindness to deal with these damned rebels. Now they will be dealt with according to their deserts."

Despite Wade's expression of confidence, most people in Washington did not know what to make of Andrew Johnson of Tennessee or what to expect from him as he faced the grave and momentous challenges before him. Johnson's background was a maze of paradoxes. He was a former tailor, raised to the highest office in the nation; a Southern politician, now in charge of the Union; and a Democrat, now head of the Republican Party (which in 1864 had been renamed the Union Party and had drafted Johnson as Lincoln's running mate in an appeal to prowar Democrats and border-state Unionists). At his March 4 swearing-in as Vice President, Johnson was suffering from the com-

bined effects of typhoid fever, a hangover, two stiff belts of whiskey and an overheated room. He had disgraced himself by delivering an incoherent inaugural address, and during his six weeks as Vice President he had kept himself in embarrassed isolation.

It was hardly an auspicious prelude to a presidency that was bound to be as historic as that of his predecessor. Lincoln had crushed the Confederacy, but it would be left to Andrew Johnson to restore the Union. On how to accomplish this daunting task, the victorious North was more deeply divided than it had ever been in wartime.

In the Republican Party alone were three discordant factions, each proposing its own program for the rebellious Southern states, each reviling the recommendations of the other two groups, yet each finding in Johnson's convoluted political record some grounds for optimism. The Radicals — Senator Wade prominent among them — wanted Confederate leaders punished as traitors, Southern states subjugated and allowed back into the Union only after a harsh and lengthy apprenticeship in loyalty, and blacks not only freed but given full rights of citizenship, including the vote. These abolitionists remembered that Johnson, in an October campaign speech to a black audience in Nashville, had promised to become the Negroes' Moses and lead them to freedom.

The moderate Republicans, largest of the party's factions, were more concerned with practical politics than with abstract princi-

The wooden cane shown above in front and side views, crafted for Andrew Johnson, symbolizes the nation's optimism as the postwar era began. The carvings include, from the top, an American bald eagle; the face of Abraham Lincoln encircled by a laurel wreath; images of Johnson and Secretary of State William Seward; and a female figure of liberty.

ples. They were not interested in punishing the leaders of secession, but they were intensely interested in preventing the return to power of the Democrats, who had once ruled the South and dominated the Congress. The moderate Republicans did not mind giving freedom to blacks, but they saw no reason to extend them the right to vote and thus muddy the country's electoral waters — unless black votes were necessary to maintain Republican dominance.

Johnson seemed to the moderates to be right on both issues. He loathed Southern planters and had supported emancipation for the same reasons that Lincoln had proposed it: to win the War and to free the slaves, with the first objective by far the more important. "Damn the Negroes," Johnson had told a Northern general, "I am fighting those traitorous aristocrats, their masters!"

Conservative Republicans, the smallest group, took a hands-off approach. The federal government had no right, they said, to dictate to any state the provisions of its constitution, concerning suffrage or any other matter. With the rebellion over and slavery outlawed, the states should simply get back to business as usual. This opinion had been shared by Secretary of State William Seward, Secretary of the Navy Gideon Welles and, seemingly, by Abraham Lincoln. Conservatives were delighted to see that Johnson soon selected former New York Senator Preston King, one of their number, as a close personal adviser.

On the opposite side of the aisle were the Northern Democrats, who had been deprived of weight and power when their party had been split in two by secession. At the War's end they held only a quarter of the seats in Congress and one Northern gover-

norship; the return of the Southern states would bring in 22 senators and 63 representatives, all of whom presumably would be Democrats. Anxious for a quick restoration of the Union on almost any terms, so that they might take center stage again, the Democrats too believed Johnson to be one of them: He had never joined the Republican Party, and with Lincoln gone he would be free to act according to his true principles.

Along with these contradictory expectations, complicated matters crowded in on President Johnson, demanding prompt action and denying him time for reflection. The slain Lincoln had to be properly buried; his assassin had to be arrested and tried; the three Confederate armies still in the field (after the surrender of Robert E. Lee's Army of Northern Virginia at Appomattox on April 9) had to be subdued; and Jefferson Davis and the other fugitive leaders of the Confederate government had to be dealt with. For a time, Johnson did not even have an office; Mrs. Lincoln, half-mad with grief, wildly accused Johnson of being involved in her husband's murder and refused to yield possession of the White House.

There was, however, no disarray in the government; the formidable Edwin M. Stanton made certain of that. Secretary of War since 1862, Stanton was a driven and competent administrator who had become one of Lincoln's closest advisers. Now he not only retained an iron grip on the minutiae of government but oversaw with grim efficiency the hunting down of John Wilkes Booth as well as anyone else suspected of conspiring in the Lincoln assassination — including Jefferson Davis, whom Stanton believed to be the mastermind behind the plot. At the same time, Stanton prepared a blueprint for dealing with the subjugated Southern states.

These plans were ready for review when Andrew Johnson convened his first Cabinet meeting on April 16 and plunged into the process begun by Lincoln that would be known to history as Reconstruction. Having tested whether the Union and slavery could endure, having confirmed the one and abolished the other, Americans now faced the problems of rebuilding their grievously wounded but still-vital country.

Questions abounded. Was the country to be ruled by a strong central government, or by the several states as had been originally conceived? Would all the states be equal in their postwar partnership, or would some, stigmatized by rebellion, be reduced to the status of territories or military departments? Were the officials of the defunct Confederate States of America to be hanged or forgiven? What was to be done with four million emancipated slaves and with the agricultural economy of the South, which seemed unable to function without slaves?

Like the Civil War itself, Reconstruction would take far longer, cause more agony and claim more lives than anyone imagined when it began. During the dozen stormy years to come, the country preserved at so great a cost would find itself riven anew: Presidents contesting with Congress, radicals arguing with conservatives, Democrats battling Republicans, blacks defending themselves from whites. Suffusing all these grim conflicts, bringing them to a boil and threatening more than once the outbreak of a new, even more savage war was the enduring hatred felt by the defeated South for the triumphant North. Ironically, while white Southerners were eventually united by their defeat into a powerful political alliance, Northerners soon

found many of the ties that had bound them together in wartime too artificial, narrow and self-serving to survive the coming of peace.

Much of the time, Reconstruction would seem less a policy than an improvisation, hesitantly shaped by men who could not agree on when to be generous, when to be punitive. The seemingly endless conflicts and compromises of the postwar years would produce mostly failure. There was, however, one remarkable success: Henceforth the term "United States" would be employed as a singular, not a plural, noun.

Jefferson Davis, President of what remained of the Confederate States of America, convened what he called a "council of war" in Abbeville, South Carolina, on the afternoon of May 2, 1865. Attended by his Secretary of War, Major General John C. Breckinridge, and his longtime friend and adviser, Major General Braxton Bragg, Davis addressed an assembly of military commanders. "It is time," he declared, "that we adopt some definite plan upon which the further prosecution of our struggle shall be conducted." He said he did not want to proceed "without the advice of my military chiefs."

The audience — five awed brigade commanders unaccustomed to conversing with the august Mr. Davis — thought he must be joking. General Lee had surrendered the Army of Northern Virginia more than three weeks earlier. A fortnight after Lee's capitulation, General Joseph E. Johnston had surrendered the Army of Tennessee in direct disobedience of Davis' orders to continue the fight. Davis himself was a fugitive, hunted by the triumphant armies of the North; he was escorted by no more than 3,000 weary and discouraged Confederate troops.

Officers of the Confederacy's Trans-Mississippi Department gathered for this photograph in June of 1865, to commemorate the wartime years they spent together. Early that month the officers had been paroled when their commander, General Edmund Kirby Smith, surrendered the South's last significant army.

Oblivious to the fact that Lee's surrender had — in almost everyone else's mind — ended the War, disgusted by Johnston's surrender of an army that was not surrounded, Davis was on his way to Alabama to join the army of Lieutenant General Richard Taylor. Davis did not know it, but on the day of his council of war, Taylor was accepting surrender terms for his army. General Edmund Kirby Smith, on the far side of the Mississippi River, would hold out just a little longer. The Southern cause was lost, and almost everyone but Jefferson Davis knew it.

The officers listening to Davis responded at first with dumfounded silence. Then,

since he asked their opinions, they told him as gently as possible that this was no temporary panic but the end of resistance. The people were broken in spirit and impoverished; the South was devastated and unable to continue the fight. The soldiers protecting him, Davis was told, intended to usher him to some safe place and then go home.

Facing reality at last, Davis rose unsteadily to his feet and said the unspeakable: "All indeed is lost." As Davis turned to leave, he stumbled, and Breckinridge stepped up to help him from the room.

Federal troops sweeping through the area were on the lookout for Davis, spurred by the knowledge that President Johnson's intentions toward him were far different from those of the late President Lincoln. Secretary of the Navy Welles wrote that at Lincoln's last Cabinet meeting, on the day he was assassinated, the President explained his attitude toward the Confederate leaders: "None need expect he would take any part in hanging or killing those men, even the worst of them. Frighten them out of the country, open the gates, let down the bars, scare them off, said he, throwing up his hands as if scaring sheep. Enough lives have been sacrificed. We must extinguish our resentments if we expect harmony and union."

But Johnson was made of sterner stuff. "Treason is a crime," he said the day after taking office as President, "and the crime must be punished. Treason must be made infamous, and traitors must be impoverished." Johnson succumbed to the fevered rumors of conspiracy afflicting official Washington, and he issued a proclamation accusing Jefferson Davis of having planned the assassination of Lincoln. The U.S. government offered $100,000 as a reward for Davis' capture.

Thus fired up, Union troopers under orders to capture or kill Jefferson Davis were approaching from every direction while the slow-moving fugitive paused near Irwinsville, Georgia, to meet his wife, who was headed for Texas with a different party of refugees. At dawn on May 10, the Confederates were surprised by a detachment of the 4th Michigan Cavalry. Davis' first thought was to escape but his hysterical wife restrained him. "God's will be done," he muttered, and surrendered with dignity.

Weary and unwell, Davis half expected to be executed. Instead he was taken to Fort Monroe in southeastern Virginia and placed in heavily guarded solitary confinement to await his destiny. It turned out to be a long wait. Harshly treated, profoundly depressed, wracked by illness, the former Confederate President languished while the Johnson Administration decided his fate.

It was a knotty problem, one that immediately became enmeshed with all the other difficulties of restoring the Union. Johnson had been anxious to capture the Confederate "traitor," but now it was Davis who was eager for a trial. Given such a forum, he could still defend the doctrine of states' rights and deny, perhaps effectively, the right of the federal government to dictate to the defeated Confederate states. Davis still believed he could prove that in seceding, he and the people of the South had asserted a constitutional right and had committed no crime. To complicate matters, the Chief Justice of the United States, Salmon P. Chase, advised the Johnson Cabinet that Davis was correct.

Unwilling to give Davis the forum he sought, Johnson left the Confederate leader to his lonely confinement and turned to the even more elusive problems of dealing with the Confederate states. The U.S. government had insisted all along that since secession was impossible, these states had never left the Union. Nevertheless, they now had to, somehow, be brought back in. Otherwise, the enormous sacrifice in blood that had just ended would have been in vain.

Leander Stillwell trudged into the village of Otterville, Illinois, one evening in the autumn of 1865 and greeted the family he had left behind when he had decided to "go for a soldier" back in 1862. As a noncommissioned officer and later as a lieutenant in

# The Embroidered Arrest of Jefferson Davis

When Jefferson Davis awoke on May 10, 1865, in a tent near Irwinsville, Georgia, he was unaware of the reward offered for his arrest or of the zealous Union troops who had surrounded his camp before dawn. Davis emerged from the tent to confront his captors wearing an overcoat and a warm shawl that his wife, Varina, had impulsively thrown over his head and shoulders; he could not have guessed that his impromptu attire would cause him to become a figure of ridicule worldwide.

Almost at once, imaginative stories began to circulate about Davis' arrest, the most persistent being that he had tried to escape in his wife's hoopskirt. Davis anguished over what was termed his "ignominious surrender," deeply resenting that anyone believed him capable of an act so "unbecoming a soldier and a gentleman."

A broadside announces the rewards offered for the capture of Jefferson Davis and five other Confederate leaders; it cites "indubitable evidence" of their involvement in the Lincoln assassination.

Northern artists delighted in the rumor that Davis was captured while disguised in his wife's clothing, and lost no time producing cartoons, *cartes de visite* and songsheets such as the one at right, showing the President of the fallen Confederacy wearing skirts and a bonnet.

# Confinement in Irons

Jefferson Davis was taken first to Federal headquarters in Macon, Georgia, then to Fort Monroe, Virginia, where he was confined in one of the fort's casemates. Armed sentries were posted inside and outside his cell; a light burned day and night so that he was always in view. Brigadier General Nelson Miles, the officer supervising Davis' incarceration, was authorized to manacle him if necessary, and on May 23, while four men restrained the enraged Davis, irons were clamped onto his legs.

At first, Northern opinion approved of the treatment, but it was soon realized that such brutal steps were unnecessary. A public outcry ensued, and by the end of May, Davis' shackles had been removed. Shortly thereafter, some concerned Northerners began engaging legal council for Davis to bring about his speedy trial.

The watercolor at top left, based on a photograph taken in the late 1860s, shows Jefferson Davis in the suit he wore when captured. "I had a waterproof raglan and a shawl about my head when I left the tent," Davis wrote, but he said that he flung them off as he approached the soldiers. Later, the shawl (*above*) and the overcoat were brought to Secretary of War Stanton, who wanted to see the "woman's dress in which Jefferson Davis was captured."

Surrounded by troopers of the 4th Michigan Cavalry, the ambulance carrying Davis and his family arrives at army headquarters in Macon, Georgia, on May 13. Varina Davis accompanied her husband to Fort Monroe, but two days later was sent with their four children to live in Savannah. Forbidden to communicate with Davis for months, his wife had news of him only through the press.

Davis, holding a copy of the Bible, sits in his Fort Monroe cell. His ever-present guards had orders not to converse with their prisoner, but to keep him in sight at all times. Unnerved by their vigilance, Davis complained to the physician who attended him, "To have a human eye riveted on you every moment is a refinement of torture on anything the Comanches or the Spanish Inquisition ever dreamed."

By Christmas of 1866, sympathy for Davis' plight was felt throughout the world; he received this crown of thorns as a gift from Pope Pius IX, who had woven it himself.

## A Trial Permanently Delayed

In 1866, Jefferson Davis was indicted for treason, but his case was not heard until May of 1867. Even then, the U.S. Attorney General was not ready for trial, and the judge released Davis on bail. Davis was never brought to trial, and on Christmas Day of 1868, by presidential proclamation, he was granted amnesty.

In anticipation of Davis' trial, the government assembled a group of white citizens and emancipated slaves (*above*) that would have become the first racially mixed petit jury in U.S. history. The jury was never called into service, however; in a crowded Richmond courtroom (*left*), Davis was set free on a $100,000 bond.

At peace at last, Jefferson Davis sits on the veranda of Beauvoir, the Mississippi estate of his old friend Mrs. Sarah Dorsey. War veterans, historians and journalists sought out Davis at Beauvoir, where he wrote his account of Southern secession, *The Rise and Fall of the Confederate Government.* It was published in 1881, eight years before he died.

Company D of the 61st Illinois Infantry, he had fought all over Arkansas and Tennessee, receiving his baptism of fire at Shiloh and nearly losing his life at Wilkinson's Pike. Stillwell's parents welcomed him without "effusive display," he recalled, and the next morning he was out in the fields with his father, cutting and shucking corn.

Tens of thousands of veterans returning home after Appomattox slipped back into civilian life as quietly as Stillwell did. As the end of 1865 approached, 800,000 men had been mustered out of the Union Army—a force that soon would number fewer than 50,000 men. The killing was over, and for some it seemed almost as if it had never happened. Leander Stillwell, for one, had the queer sensation as he stood in the family cornfield that he "had been away only a day or two, and had just taken up the farm work where I had left off."

Yet Stillwell and thousands of others had changed in ways they scarcely understood. The men of the North and South had fought 10,455 major and minor engagements and had suffered more than a million casualties. Aside from the dead—360,222 from all causes on the Union side and an estimated 258,000 on the Confederate side—there were the countless thousands who bore the marks of the War. According to the official records, at least 280,000 Union veterans returned home with wounds of varying severity; the Confederate wounded came to somewhat more than half that number. But the records had nothing to say about the hidden casualties of the War: those who came home mentally crippled or so debilitated physically that their health would remain precarious for the rest of their days.

Many of the men who returned intact had changed in subtler ways. Leander Stillwell would soon find farm life too confining; after taking a degree in law, he would embark on a distinguished career as a legislator and judge. Others would wander west, moved both by the promise of riches and by an ill-defined restlessness that was part of their heritage from the War.

The idealism that had driven many men into the army was noticeably lacking among the returning veterans: "I am not the same man," Oliver Wendell Holmes Jr. warned his blue-blooded Bostonian parents as he left the army in 1864 and began on a legal career. By his own admission, Holmes had changed from a crusader into a pragmatist who did not "acknowledge the same claims upon me" that had existed at the outbreak of war. Like many others in the North, he had a diminished sense of divine purpose and an increased respect for the uses of power.

The society to which the veterans returned was throbbing with such power. The War had helped turn the Northern states into an industrial society whose potential was unleashed by the coming of peace. Steel, oil, gold and silver mining, railroad construction—all expanded on an unprecedented scale. The industrial ferment launched the nation on the path that would lead to modern America and changed the way Americans viewed their lives. Looking back from the vantage point of the 1870s, Pennsylvania Congressman William D. Kelley recalled that when the guns fell silent, "The American people waked each morning to feel that there were great duties before them." There were "mines to be opened, forges and furnaces to be erected, new houses to be built: Our wealth grew as it had never grown."

Such was not the case in the South, which

was wracked by physical devastation, social dislocation and fears of the sort expressed by a young Georgia woman that "the most terrible part of the war is now to come." Among Southern blacks there was the promise — and also the peril — of freedom.

In July of 1865, the German-born Republican politician Carl Schurz traveled through the Southern states at Johnson's request and came back shocked by what he had seen. The interior of South Carolina, he reported, "looked for many miles like a broad black streak of ruin and desolation — the fences all gone; lonesome smoke stacks, surrounded by dark heaps of ashes and cinders, marking the spots where human habitations had stood; the fields along the road wildly overgrown by weeds, with here and there a sickly looking patch of cotton or corn cultivated by Negro squatters."

No one who visited the post-Civil War South could fail to be impressed by its poverty and its physical devastation. Much of Atlanta, Columbia, Charleston, Richmond and Mobile was in ruins. The Shenandoah Valley and the Valley of the Tennessee had been laid waste. A Northern journalist named John Townsend Trowbridge found farmers plowing among corpses, homeless families sheltering in hovels and impoverished women scavenging the battlefields for old bullets and scrap metal to sell. Hogs rooted among the graves, and dead horses and mules lay rotting in the sun because there were no shovels with which to bury them.

Material losses were enormous. The emancipation of the slaves had removed some two billion dollars from the balance sheets of the planters and farmers who had owned them. In addition, the Confederate states owed $712 million in war debts and had lost untold millions in the destruction of property, livestock, crops, industrial plants and transport. It would take more than 25 years to replace the lost horses, mules, oxen, cattle and hogs, and almost that long to return farm production to its prewar levels.

The railroad system of the South had almost ceased to exist. Travelers found rails wrapped around trees, crossties burned, freight and passenger cars wrecked, creeks and rivers without trestles. Mills and factories had been dismantled, mines shut down and insurance companies bankrupted. The collapse of the Confederate monetary and credit system had wiped out private savings and forced the banks to close.

People scrabbled for a living in any way they could. Landowners who had never held a job took positions as clerks and farmhands or joined the crews laboring to repair the ruined railroads. The New York *Tribune's* James Shepherd Pike came across a ramshackle South Carolina mansion occupied by the sole survivor of one of the richest families in the state. Pike reported that the man earned his living peddling "tea by the pound and molasses by the quart, on a corner of the old homestead, to the former slaves of the family."

There were no brass bands to greet the Confederate soldiers returning to this blighted land. Seeing "the shattered remains of Lee's army" come streaming through central and northern Georgia, young Eliza Andrews was struck by their "ragged, starving, hopeless, reckless" air.

Anarchy was everywhere, noted Emma Holmes of South Carolina, with "villages sacked in Yankee style by lawless mobs, and every man returning from the army on mule or horse having to guard his animals & him-

Wagons from General Sherman's army head down the muddy main street of Zanesville, Ohio, in June of 1865. The remnants of Sherman's quartermaster and commissary trains were driven west and distributed among U.S. Army posts on the frontier.

self with loaded weapons." Roaming outlaw bands plundered and terrorized their countrymen, stealing cotton, horses and cattle, even household effects. In the summer of 1865, a certain "Major" Perry became notorious in rural Alabama as the leader of a gang that went from house to house demanding valuables from occupants and pillaging trunks and wardrobes.

The only law enforcement in the postwar South was provided by federal troops, who at their peak numbered 200,000. Military courts were charged with holding trials and punishing criminals. In response to immediate civilian needs, federal relief commissions were established in a number of cities. Often they were under the auspices of the Bureau of Freedmen, Refugees and Abandoned Lands, an organization created by Congress on March 3, 1865, to feed and care for Southern refugees both black and white. Because blacks could not testify against whites in most Southern courts, the Freedmen's Bureau set up courts of its own to adjudicate in such cases. As well, during the summer of 1865, the Freedmen's Bureau issued 150,000 rations every day — a third of them to whites — and the army issued rations as well. In the generosity thus expressed, noted a Confederate veteran, "there is much that takes away the bitter sting."

Nevertheless, loathing of the North was widespread and unrelenting. A Savannah woman taught her children never to utter the word "Yankee" without adding the epithets "hateful" and "thieving." A North Carolina innkeeper told a Northern journalist that the Yankees had killed his sons, burned his house and stolen his slaves, leaving him only with the privilege of venting his spleen: "I git up at half-past four in the morning,

and sit up till twelve at night, to hate 'em."

There were more moderate voices, of course, and even some who saw defeat as liberation from the responsibility and guilt that slave-owning imposed. A planter's wife remarked that Mr. Lincoln had set her free, and the *Southern Cultivator* editorialized in July of 1865 that "the Law which freed the Negro at the same time freed the master."

But this was a view not held by the majority. Most Southerners remained not only bitter about the Yankees but resentful and fearful of the emancipated blacks. Mary Chesnut of South Carolina recorded in her journal a troubling story about a planter who had returned to his plantation at the end of the War to be told politely but firmly by his former slaves, "We own this land now: Put it out of your head that it will ever be yours again."

There was fear that blacks were planning the murder of whites, and a deep reluctance

In a painting honoring the event, color-bearers from every Massachusetts regiment mount the steps to the Statehouse in December 1865, to present their battle flags to Governor John A. Andrew. "Proud memories of many fields," said Andrew, "twine around these splintered staves, weave themselves along these familiar flags, war worn, begrimed and baptized with blood."

to accept the reality of emancipation. A Tennessee politician, Emerson Etheridge, spoke for many Southern whites when he said that "The Negroes are no more free than they were forty years ago, and if anyone goes about the country telling them that they are free, shoot him."

For the blacks, the moment was laden with hope but it was also enormously difficult. They responded to the news of emancipation with outbursts of joy in some cases and with remarkable restraint in others. Some of them thought freedom meant permission to evict their master from the big house and move in; they felt that the property belonged to those whose labor had created the wealth. Many others grasped their first opportunity to travel, and for months after Appomattox thousands of blacks wandered the roads in a restless migration. Some were looking for family members who had been sold to distant plantations. Others found their way to the cities in quest of jobs, schools or government food and clothing.

In at least one sense, blacks had an edge on Southern whites: They were accustomed to backbreaking labor and to surviving on very little. Yet the former slaves were entering a daunting world without adequate preparation. "The emancipated slaves own nothing," noted a leading Tennessee planter, "because nothing but freedom has been given them." Few blacks had the education, skills or experience to cope with their sudden independence. About 97 percent of them were illiterate; many had never eaten with utensils, bought a railroad ticket or used money. Watching a group of freed slaves being paid on a plantation, Northern journalist Whitelaw Reid was struck by the way they handled the money "as if it were fragile glass" and examined it "with a puzzled air."

Some blacks made ends meet by selling stolen goods to unscrupulous white merchants who accepted such goods in exchange for groceries, trinkets and liquor. The majority of former slaves who went to work for wages often were exploited by plantation stores where they could buy, at exorbitant prices, a variety of alluring articles that were charged against their future pay. In the beginning they had only the sketchiest notion of the value of the goods they bought relative to the wages due them.

The most persistent rumor in black communities was that freed slaves were to share in the division of their former masters' lands. Merchants sold them little red, white and blue pegs, explaining that they were to be used to stake out the lands they claimed as their own. This dream of possessing "40 acres and a mule" was more than a delusion. Indeed, by June of 1865 the federal government had relocated nearly 10,000 families on half a million acres of land abandoned by planters who had fled Union armies along the coastal rivers of Georgia and South Carolina. Moreover, powerful Republicans in Washington were threatening to "strip the proud nobility" in the South "of their bloated estates," and to redistribute the land.

Yet for many blacks the changes were too great and too confusing to cope with. Thousands of them had no real choice but to stay on as hired hands or sharecroppers on the plantations where they were born, glad, as one of them put it, "to have a cabin to live in and a place to farm on."

The political fate of the South had been a concern of the U.S. government almost from the time the War began. Lincoln had spoken of it to Congress as early as 1861, and had begun his program of reconstruction as soon as portions of the seceded states had fallen under Northern control. His aim was to get the states into "their proper practical relation with the Union" as rapidly as possible and with minimum government intervention. He proposed to grant a general amnesty to all who would take an oath of allegiance to the United States, high-ranking officers of the Confederacy excepted. Beyond that, he would accept any state in which 10 percent of the voters of 1860 — that is, the white voters — had taken such an oath.

Lincoln laid out his program in the Proclamation of Amnesty and Reconstruction on December 8, 1863. That document proved to be too liberal for the Congress, which in July of 1864 adopted a bill introduced by Senator Wade and Maryland Representative Henry Winter Davis. The Wade-Davis bill differed from Lincoln's initiative in several ways. It required 50 percent of the voters, rather than only 10 percent, to pledge allegiance to the Union; it provided for military governors to rule the Confederate states until state conventions had drafted new constitutions repudiating secession and refusing to pay Confederate war debts, and abolishing slavery. And it enfranchised only those white males who took an "ironclad" oath that they had never willingly supported the South.

This legislation raised two difficult questions: whether the federal government had the right to dictate to any state the articles of its constitution; and whether the restoration of the Union was the responsibility of the executive or legislative branch of the government. Lincoln pocket-vetoed the bill as improperly dictatorial and proceeded to set up loyalist governments in the states of Lou-

isiana, Arkansas, Virginia and Tennessee. The executive-legislative confrontation of Lincoln's last months in office would return to haunt the Administration of the man who succeeded him. Andrew Johnson's background was not unlike Lincoln's — they both came out of poor rural environments — but Johnson's years of struggle had left him embittered and suspicious. His animus was particularly directed at the South's planter aris-

tocracy. These were the men, he believed, who exploited the poor whites of the South and held them in contempt. He made a vow that some day he would "show the stuck-up aristocrats who is running the country. A cheap, purse-proud set they are, not half as good as the man who earns his bread by the sweat of his brow."

Johnson's rise had been one of the most remarkable in American politics. Brought up in North Carolina with no formal schooling, he had remained largely illiterate until, at the age of 18, he had moved to Tennessee, set himself up as a tailor and married a shoemaker's daughter who taught him to write. Thanks to native intelligence and a devotion to hard work, he had prospered; and he entered local politics as a Democrat.

Johnson's constituents, then and later, were the white owners of small farms, whose interests were often opposed to those of the large planters. With the farmers' backing he had climbed the political ladder — alderman, mayor, state legislator, congressman, governor — and at the outbreak of the Civil War he had been the only Southern senator who did not abandon his seat. This, together with his demonstrated appeal to Democratic voters and his successful governorship of occupied Tennessee, where he introduced emancipation, had earned him his place on the 1864 ticket with Lincoln.

The Radicals were much heartened by Johnson's vengeful pursuit of Jefferson Davis, but as the new President grappled with the intricacies of Reconstruction it soon became clear that his sympathies were mixed. He was ambivalent about giving blacks the vote, saying bluntly that former slaves had little capacity for self-government and that he was not out to "Africanize the South." He doubted that the black and white races could or should live together on an equal footing.

In these attitudes, Johnson reflected his Southern background and perhaps also the influence of a Cabinet, inherited from Lincoln, that tended to be sympathetic to the South. Two of the strongest Cabinet figures, Secretary of the Navy Welles and Secretary of State Seward, were firmly for states' rights and were notably unsympathetic to black as-

An 1865 photograph of burned-out buildings in Columbia, South Carolina, only hints at the full measure of the city's destruction. A journalist called Columbia "a wilderness of ruins. Its heart is but a mass of blackened chimneys and crumbling walls." Nearly two thirds of the capital was in ashes; it was the worst devastation inflicted on any city during the War.

pirations. Secretary of War Stanton was the only influential Cabinet officer who favored black suffrage.

When Johnson's plan of Reconstruction — which he preferred to call "restoration" — was made public in May, it turned out to be far more liberal than the Radicals had anticipated. On May 29, Johnson issued two proclamations. The first granted pardons and returned property to virtually all who would take an oath of allegiance — although former Confederate government officials, officers of high rank and owners of more than $20,000 worth of property had to apply to him personally for individual pardons. The second proclamation appointed a provisional governor in North Carolina and instructed him to call an election of delegates to frame a new state constitution. The delegates were responsible for establishing permanent voting and officeholding qualifications for the state. Before doing so, however, they were required to adopt and fulfill certain other obligations: most notably, the ratification of the 13th Amendment, ending slavery. The provisional governor was temporarily in charge of the state's civil government while federal responsibilities, such as collecting tariffs and delivering the mail, were to be resumed by the proper officials. During the next several weeks, Johnson issued similar proclamations affecting six other Confederate states. He also recognized the Lincoln-sponsored governments of Louisiana, Arkansas and Tennessee and the loyalist government that had presided over the Union-occupied portion of Virginia.

Significantly, Johnson's plan specified that only white voters loyal to the Union could take part in the constitutional conventions, and that the conventioners themselves would have the power to determine the qualifications of voters within the state. The net effect was to offer Southerners rapid control of their state governments and to guarantee them a South ruled by whites.

Early in June, news of Johnson's proclamations reached the manorial home of Colonel Thomas H. Carter, a former Confederate artillerist, in King William County, Virginia. Carter was interested in the details, of course, but not with the intensity of his visiting cousin from Richmond — Robert E. Lee.

It was Lee's first excursion from Richmond since his surrender. Alone, on his famous gray horse Traveller, he had ridden to the Carter house over fields still scarred by the death struggle of his army. For several days he took his ease, watching Traveller graze in lush pastures, talking about family affairs and a farm he might buy, playing for hours with the Carters' three- and five-year-old daughters. Lee's son Robert E. Lee Jr. wrote later that "the days passed here were the happiest he had spent for many years."

But Johnson's amnesty proclamation meant that the weary Lee must make one more fateful decision. Its terms required him, along with other ex-Confederates of rank, to apply to the President for a pardon. Although Johnson made it clear that he would grant such requests readily, many Southern leaders abhorred the prospect of asking forgiveness for something they did not believe had been wrong. Lee knew that most would look to him to set the example, and he felt the responsibility keenly.

It seemed to Lee that Johnson's offer was more than fair. The Confederacy was lost, and the federal government had the power to impose its will on the South. But instead of

Returning Confederate soldiers, like the one in this contemporary painting, faced bleak prospects — ravaged homes, barren land, financial ruin. A South Carolina planter described the task of rebuilding that lay ahead: "We are discouraged," he said, "we have nothing left to begin anew with. I never did a day's work in my life, and don't know how to begin."

harsh retribution, it offered immediate restoration of personal freedom, property rights, self-government — and white rule. One had only to ask, and Robert E. Lee, having no false pride, was ready to do so. He mounted Traveller and, much refreshed and encouraged, returned to Richmond.

Lee's reaction was probably the most favorable one received by Johnson's reconstruction program, and it was not well rewarded. On arriving in Richmond, Lee learned that he had been indicted for treason. He did not want to appear to be avoiding trial, so he made his application for pardon conditional on not being prosecuted. The matter sank into limbo, and during Lee's lifetime he was neither tried nor pardoned.

Congress was in recess when Johnson unveiled his plan, so its members for the time being could only fume from the sidelines. Fume they did. It seemed to the Radical Republicans that Johnson was giving away the victory won by the North. "This Republic cannot be lost," ranted Senator Charles Sumner of Massachusetts, "but the President has done much to lose it." Congressman Thaddeus Stevens of Pennsylvania asked his colleagues if there were "no way to arrest the insane course of the President." Neither Sumner nor Stevens wanted to see the Republicans lose their majority to a resurgent South allied with Northern Democrats.

Unexpectedly, emancipation had brought the Southern bloc greater potential power in national politics. The Constitution had specified that slaves be counted as three fifths of a person for purposes of representation; now each black person would be counted as one. As a result the South would have a dozen more congressmen — ensuring Southern whites an increase in proportionate representation that could be offset only by the enfranchisement of blacks.

Johnson's generous terms encouraged many people in the South to believe that they could live as they had before the War and, in the words of a New Orleans citizen, "put an end to the career of nigger agitators." The new state constitutions drafted at Johnson's direction made no effort to give the vote to freedmen, and the new state legislatures began rushing through discriminatory laws designed to preserve white supremacy.

These Black Codes, as they came to be known, varied from state to state and even from town to town, but all of them severely circumscribed black social, economic and political rights. In the town of Opelousas, Louisiana, for example, blacks could not live within the town limits unless they worked for a white person, or enter the town without permission from their employers, or remain on the streets after ten at night. Blacks could not own weapons — in Florida the penalty was "thirty-nine lashes on the bare back" — and they needed special permission to preach or to engage in commerce.

In most states, vagrancy, or lack of "visible means of support," was treated as a crime to be punished by six months to a year of forced labor. In Louisiana, agricultural workers lost wages for the days they were sick and double the amount if the sickness was thought to be feigned. Blacks were barred from white transport facilities, and both black and white participants in interracial marriages could be sent to prison for life. On a variety of pretexts, blacks — particularly those under 18 — could be hired out to the highest bidder. A delegation of blacks who came to see Chief Justice Salmon Chase while he was on a Southern tour told him that slavery to all intents still existed.

When Congress reconvened in December, representatives of eight Southern states that had met Johnson's conditions for readmission to the Union demanded to be seated. Among them were many leading military and political figures of the war years, including newly elected Georgia Senator Alexander H. Stephens, who, as Vice President of the Confederacy, had declared that for the black man "slavery — subordination to the superi-

or race — is his natural and normal condition." Democrats were delighted and claimed Johnson for their own. But the appalled Republican majority barred all of the Southerners and appointed a committee to draft an alternative reconstruction program.

Meantime, the docility shown by former Confederates immediately after the War was giving way to a new aggressiveness. This change became particularly noticeable during the summer of 1866, after large numbers of Federal troops had been withdrawn from the South. In Memphis, a fight broke out between police and discharged black soldiers. After six blacks and two policemen had been shot, the chief of police told his men to "kill the last damned one of the nigger race, and burn up the cradle." Police and local toughs rampaged through black neighborhoods, killing 46 people and burning to the ground 90 houses and a dozen schools. A city newspaper commented approvingly, "Thank heaven the white race are once more rulers of Memphis."

In New Orleans, blacks gathering for a suffrage convention were attacked by a mob led by the sheriff, who was a former Confederate general. When the blacks hid in the convention hall, the mob — augmented by police — rushed in, firing indiscriminately. The death toll was 37 blacks and three of their white allies; hundreds were wounded.

Both riots received wide publicity in the North: They demonstrated, suggested the New York *Tribune* sarcastically, what blacks might expect from "the paternal care of their old masters." The *Tribune's* Whitelaw Reid noted that there were also daily, random acts of violence that went largely unnoticed. In Salisbury, North Carolina, he found a young white woman named Temple Neeley — one

Terrified black men, women and children flee from armed whites during the Memphis riots in early May of 1866. The three days of violence, triggered by a quarrel between black veterans of the Federal Army and local police, resulted in the indiscriminate killing of 46 blacks by gangs of whites.

Three months after the carnage in Memphis, blacks marching to a suffrage assembly in New Orleans were assaulted by angry white citizens and police (*foreground*). Federal troops stationed three miles outside the city were alerted immediately, but by the time they arrived the clash was almost over and 40 people were dead.

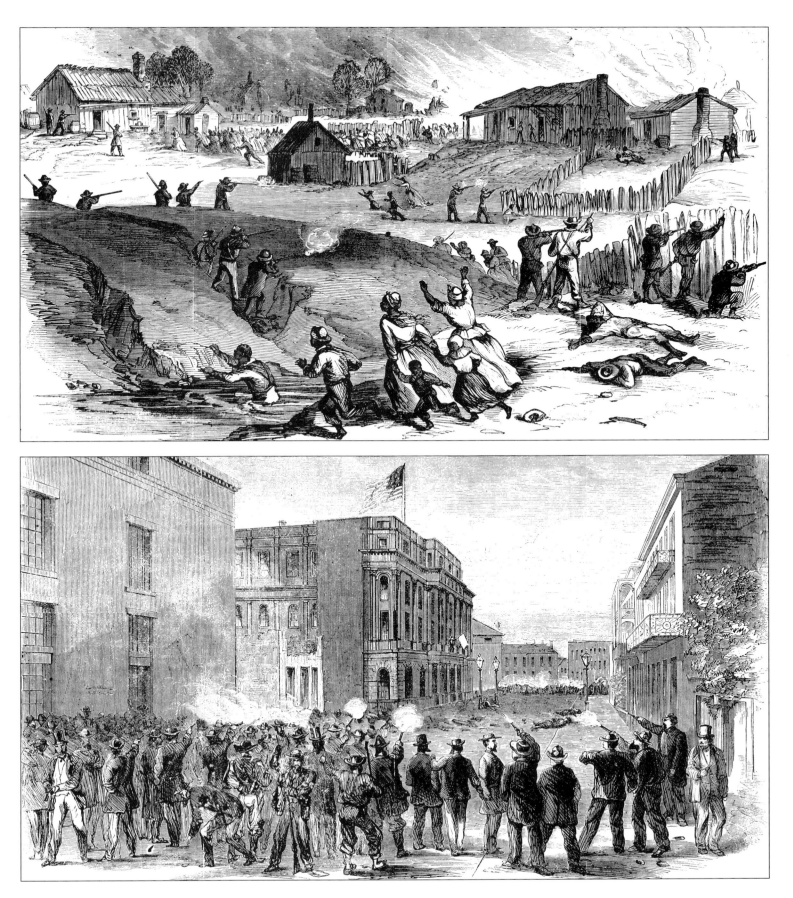

of "the wealthiest, most refined and respectable young ladies" in the county — charged with shooting a black mother who had tried to protect her child from a whipping. In Jackson County, Florida, a young black was shot for not pulling his cart to the side of the road quickly enough, and in New Orleans a freedman was shot for refusing to take off his hat in the presence of his former master.

Even more disturbing to Northerners was the birth of organized intimidation of blacks and Unionists, as practiced by the Ku Klux Klan, the Knights of the White Camelia, the Sons of Midnight and various other quasimilitary organizations. The best known of these, the Ku Klux Klan, was founded in December 1865 in Pulaski, Tennessee, by a group of unemployed Confederate veterans, among whom was the famed cavalry leader Nathan Bedford Forrest. Garbed in hooded robes or white bedsheets, Klansmen tried to frighten blacks into submission or flight by paying midnight visits in the guise of the ghosts of dead Confederate soldiers. If the warnings failed, the Klan resorted to violence — crippling whippings and beatings, or "execution" by shooting or hanging. The aim, said a Klan paper in Alabama, was to "kill or drive away leading Negroes and only let the humble and submissive remain." The Klan soon counted many leading landowners among its "Grand Dragons" and "Grand Titans," and had sufficient rank-and-file strength to mount a parade of 1,500 Klansmen in Huntsville, Alabama.

In the fearful climate of the postwar South, even comparatively liberal Southerners such as Elizabeth Avery Meriwether of Memphis welcomed the appearance of the Klan as a "miracle." Meanwhile, a black minister in Washington, Henry Turner,

charged Johnson with "the murder of thousands of our people." Alarmed both by Johnson's reconstruction plan and by the rising tide of violence, the Joint Committee on Reconstruction began Congressional hearings early in 1866 to determine the situation in the South. Witnesses told of assaults on the black community and seizure of black property, coupled with an intense resentment of blacks that had prompted one elderly Southerner to remark: "If you take away the military from Tennessee, the buzzards can't eat up the niggers as fast as we'll kill 'em." The publication of such testimony led to a hardening of Northern attitudes and demands for a tougher policy toward the South.

Further inflaming the public and Republican legislators was Johnson's decision in February 1866 to veto a bill extending the life of the Freedmen's Bureau, which was due to expire. To moderate Republicans, the bureau seemed an essential instrument for the protection of black rights. Under the conscientious Major General Oliver O. Howard, the bureau had expanded its activities far beyond emergency relief and arbitration between blacks and whites.

The Freedmen's Bureau negotiated black wages and conditions of labor, provided transportation to new homes and places of employment, and established schools and hospitals for blacks. In some instances, the bureau was responsible for setting up entire black communities. In addition, after Congress passed the Southern Homestead Act of 1866, which offered black and Unionist white homesteaders the first crack at 44 million acres of public land, in tracts of 80 acres, the Freedmen's Bureau offered one-month subsistence grants to help defray the initial cost of establishing a farm. But the land

# Andersonville Avenged

Among the Union soldiers finding their way home in the spring of 1865 were the survivors of Confederate prison camps, many of them carrying tales of starvation and brutality. The largest of the Southern prisons was at Andersonville, Georgia; stories of atrocities there made Andersonville synonymous with hell.

The camp's commandant, Captain Henry Wirz, became the target of Northern rage. Wirz was arrested and brought before a military tribunal in Washington, where he was charged with conspiring to "injure the health and destroy the lives" of Union soldiers, and with "murder in violation of the laws and customs of war."

For 63 days, 148 witnesses told of Wirz's misdeeds. Evidence presented in his defense was passed over lightly, and on October 24, Wirz was found guilty and sentenced to hang (*following pages*).

Captain Henry Wirz (*above*), the Swiss-born commandant of Andersonville, served nine years in various European armies before migrating to Louisiana. He joined the Confederate Army, and in 1862 suffered wounds that left him in almost constant pain. He was assigned to Andersonville in 1864.

Newspaper reporters assemble at the steps leading from the Old Capitol Prison in Washington to witness the hanging of the man they had labeled "the Andersonville savage."

# A Hanging on Capitol Hill

President Johnson received several pleas to spare Henry Wirz's life, including one from the consul general of Wirz's native Switzerland. Wirz "was only the detestable tool of monsters in human form," the diplomat asserted. "Shall the hand suffer for the arm that wielded it?"

Johnson stood firm, however, and on November 10, 1865, Wirz climbed a scaffold erected near the U.S. Capitol. After the court's findings were read aloud, he turned to the officer in charge of the execution and said, "I know what orders are, Major. I am being hanged for obeying them."

Captain Henry Wirz stands on the scaffold as his death warrant is read. The only Confederate to be executed for war crimes, Wirz maintained his innocence to the end. "I go before my God," he declared, "and He will judge between me and you."

To the jeers of soldiers lining the prison wall and spectators perched in nearby trees, the scaffold's trap door springs open and Wirz drops to his death. He was buried in the yard of the Washington Arsenal, alongside the four conspirators hanged earlier that year for their roles in the assassination of President Lincoln.

proved inferior and the grants too small; few of the homesteads were claimed.

Southern whites complained angrily that the Freedmen's Bureau was simply an agency for the perpetuation of Republican rule over the South. Although there were many charges of corruption and graft in the conduct of bureau affairs, Johnson was more concerned with what he regarded as a serious challenge to civil law in the South. In the exercise of its judicial powers, he argued, the bureau was applying war powers in a time of peace. The President's concern was shared by the Supreme Court, which ruled in a separate case that a citizen could not be tried by a military tribunal once the civil courts were open. Moreover, nothing in the Constitution anticipated a "system for the support of indigent persons."

Johnson's critics considered his veto a capitulation to the worst racist elements in the South and a cynical renunciation of federal concern for blacks. From now on, predicted moderate Republican Senator Lyman Trumbull of Illinois, author of the bill, the freed slave would be "tyrannized over, abused and virtually reenslaved without some legislation for his protection."

The Democrats, on the other hand, were elated by Johnson's veto, and they held a number of mass meetings in Washington to give endorsement to his stand. On Washington's birthday, a mere three days after the veto, 6,000 participants at a Democratic rally marched to the White House and serenaded the President. Johnson received them with evident delight. He then delivered a rambling, disjointed speech that lasted more than an hour and shocked Northern opinion. The Radicals had become traitors, Johnson strongly implied — he compared them to Judas Iscariot and likened himself to Christ.

A voice in the crowd called out, "Give us the names." Carried away, Johnson replied: "I say Thaddeus Stevens of Pennsylvania, I say Charles Sumner of Massachusetts, I say Wendell Phillips of Massachusetts and others of the same stripe." As the applause mounted, Johnson evidently envisioned himself a martyr selected for assassination by his Radical enemies. "If my blood is to be shed because I vindicate the Union," he cried, "let it be shed."

Later, George Templeton Strong, a prominent New York attorney, remarked dryly in his diary that the "bouquet" of the speech was "that of Old Bourbon, largely imbibed by the orator just before taking the rostrum." Even the President's supporters now began to draw away from him in alarm. Senator William Pitt Fessenden of Maine, the chairman of the Joint Committee on Reconstruction, declared that Johnson had "broken the faith" and "must sink from detestation to contempt."

President Johnson's veto was sustained. By now, relations between the executive and legislative branches had become nearly deadlocked, with the President insisting on the validity of the all-white state governments his reconstruction plan had created and Congress denying their legality. Initially, the staunchly conservative judicial branch stood closer to Johnson in its attitudes and was markedly unsympathetic to the punitive legislation favored by the Radical Republicans. In two separate decisions, the Supreme Court called into question the constitutionality of loyalty oaths and the right of military courts to bring civilians to trial when the civil courts were functioning. The administration of military justice in the South, said the

Court severely, was "mere lawless violence."

These opinions infuriated Radicals, for they drew attention to obvious abuses in a system where normal judicial safeguards did not apply and the writ of habeas corpus could be suspended at the whim of the occupying forces. Radical orators and editors denounced the high court for "judicial impertinence" and for meddling in the affairs of Congress. Men like Wendell Phillips and Congressman John A. Bingham of Ohio, who was generally counted a moderate, even threatened the court's abolition. Nothing came of that particular threat, but Congress did succeed later in overriding a presidential veto to forbid the Supreme Court to hear appeals from the military courts established by the forces of occupation. The Court itself bowed to Congress by holding that the legislative branch had a right to define and limit the jurisdiction of the judicial branch. To some, this yield to Radical pressure seemed to threaten the system of tripartite government. Moderate Republican Senator Orville H. Browning of Illinois termed the Court's acquiescence "cowardice" and "among the alarming symptoms of the times."

The refusal of the justices to take a firm stand was a blow to Johnson, who had counted on the Court's record of sympathy toward the South. Increasingly, the President found himself isolated. Partly in reaction to Johnson's intemperate Washington's birthday attack on the Radicals, Congress in March of 1866 passed a civil rights bill by an overwhelming majority. Conceived and introduced by Illinois' Senator Trumbull, the bill was designed to guarantee federal protection for freed slaves and to invalidate the Black Codes. For the first time in American legislative history, it asserted the right of the feder-

Congressman Thaddeus Stevens of Pennsylvania, an outspoken Radical Republican, abhorred Andrew Johnson's leniency toward the South and his evident unconcern for the rights of blacks. Stevens pressed for laws to "revolutionize Southern institutions, habits, and manners. The foundations," he said, "must be broken up and relaid, or all our blood and treasure have been spent in vain."

al government to intervene in state affairs to protect the rights of citizens. The legislation also provided the first national definition of citizenship, as applying to all persons born in the United States, untaxed Indians excluded. The new law would thus clearly confer citizenship on blacks. All citizens, the bill added, had equal rights regardless of race.

Moderates and every member of the Cabinet, with the exception of Gideon Welles, advised Johnson to sign the Civil Rights Act. Stubbornly, he insisted on vetoing it. Not only did the bill infringe on states' rights, he declared, but by giving blacks immediate citizenship it discriminated against foreigners who were required to wait five years to become citizens. Finally, he said, it gave a degree of federal protection to blacks that whites did not enjoy and was thus discriminatory against the white race.

Johnson's veto message, sent to the Congress on March 27, 1866, drew cheers once again from the Democrats. It was clear, said a Democratic editor, that Johnson did not believe "in compounding our race with niggers, gipsies, and baboons." But at the same time the civil rights veto, more than any other single act of the President's, served to drive moderate Republicans into the ranks of the Radicals. Congressman Henry L. Dawes of Massachusetts, who had defended Johnson against his harshest critics, now wrote to his wife that the President had deprived "every friend he has of the least ground upon which to stand and defend him."

Within three weeks of the Johnson veto, moderates joined Radicals to override it by one vote. A few weeks after that, a newly defiant Congress passed a second Freedmen's Bureau bill and pushed it through against a second presidential veto. The Republican Congress had served notice that Reconstruction as conceived by the President and the Democrats was finished. The future course of reuniting the nation would be determined by the legislative branch — the Republican Senate and House.

# Free—but Far from Equal

"We are engaged in a stubborn war with unrelenting foes, which we mean to fight to the end on our native soil, aiming to complete the establishment of our rights and liberties," former slave Henry H. Garnett told an audience of freedmen and women in 1866. "Our weapons are the spelling book, the Bible, the press and the implements of industry; our impregnable fortifications are schoolhouses and the Church."

For most blacks, life after slavery was indeed a war of sorts. Impoverished in everything except will power, without even a family name, they had emerged from 250 years of bondage into a society that considered them fit only for hard labor. With the help of the Freedmen's Bureau and Northern missionary societies, the former slaves began pulling themselves up by their bootstraps. But they quickly learned a bitter truth: Freedom in no sense meant equality.

Blacks' hopes to own their own farms collided head on with the interests of their former masters. When the U.S. Government returned to the planters their confiscated estates, the majority of freedmen found themselves back on the plantation, working in virtual peonage. The black slogan "Forty acres and a mule" had been replaced, a Kentucky newspaper reported, with the white warning, "Work nigger, or starve!"

"We thought we was going to be richer than the white folks, 'cause we was stronger and knowed how to work," a former slave said. "We soon found out that freedom could make folks proud, but it didn't make 'em rich."

In a weed-choked cornfield, a black couple demonstrates how freed slaves plowed their land without a mule or horse. Ten years after emancipation, barely 5 percent of the former slaves owned their own land, and those who did lacked the capital and credit to develop it.

## A New Kind of Bondage

"Freedom wasn't no difference I knows of," lamented a former slave. "I works for Marse John just the same." For many blacks, life had changed little. They lived on the same plantation and toiled under the same overseer — only now for a meager wage or a modest share of the crop.

In the new labor contracts signed by blacks, planters often inserted the clause, "to work in the same manner as always," and even the most humane planter expected to be treated with nothing less than complete deference. "He wishes still to be master," noted a postwar traveler in Virginia, "is willing to be a kind master, but will never be a just employer."

Laborers on a South Carolina cotton plantation bring in the day's pickings. Many of the former slaves were hired as family units.

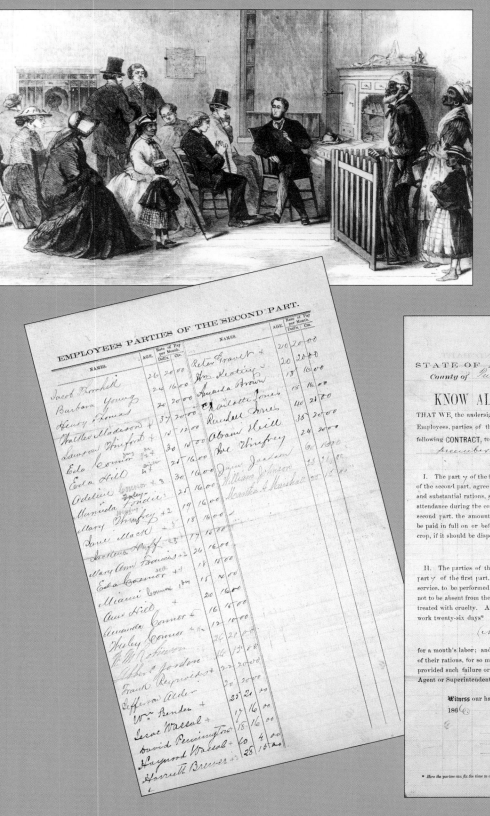

A Freedmen's Bureau official in Richmond settles a dispute between a black family (*in the witness box at right*) and their employer. "Men who are honorable in their dealings with white neighbors," said one official, "will cheat a Negro without feeling a single twinge of their honor."

In this one-year labor contract, an Arkansas planter agreed to provide workers with a monthly wage plus food, fuel and living quarters. "The contract system has succeeded in making labor secure and stable," a Freedmen's Bureau official wrote. "But it has failed to secure the freedman his just compensation."

## An Ardent Affirming of Family Ties

A powerful sense of family was all that most freedmen carried with them out of slavery. Thousands of couples had their marriages, begun in servitude, sanctified by clergymen or by government officials.

Members of families that had been torn asunder by sale scoured the countryside looking for their relatives. "Every mother's son seemed to be in search of his mother," a Freedmen's Bureau agent in South Carolina reported in 1865, "every mother in search of her children." But for most, it was a needle-in-a-haystack endeavor. Two decades after the War, black newspapers were still full of queries from ex-slaves seeking long-lost loved ones.

Black families begin the day in front of the same cabins they had occupied as slaves. "Everything happened in that one room — birth, sickness, death."

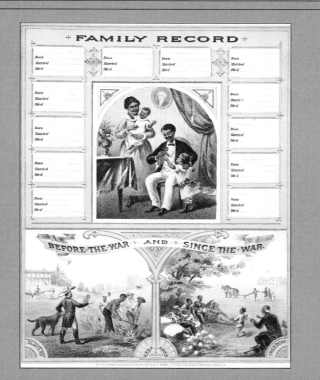

This family record, reflecting the visions of Northern idealists, was meant to help blacks keep track of births, deaths and marriages after emancipation. Most slaves had only given names; out of expediency, many freedmen assumed their master's surname. "It was the easiest way to be identified," one ex-slave said.

A black soldier and his sweetheart are wed by a Freedmen's Bureau chaplain at Vicksburg, Mississippi. Many black soldiers asked that the unions they had made while slaves be legalized by the federal government so that in case of their deaths, their wives and children would qualify for survivor benefits.

# "A Whole Race Going to School"

In 1865, fewer than 150,000 of the four million freed slaves in the United States were literate. Convinced that to remain in ignorance was to remain in bondage, tens of thousands of them attended schools organized by the Freedmen's Bureau. "It was a whole race trying to go to school," wrote ex-slave and future educator Booker T. Washington. "Few were too young, and none too old to make an attempt to learn."

At first, most of the teachers in black schools were white Northern missionaries — a fact that infuriated Southern whites. "Ostracism is a mild term for the disesteem with which they were regarded," one observer declared. " 'Nigger teachers' was one of the most opprobrious epithets that the Southern vocabulary furnished."

A teacher assembles her charges outside their school in North Carolina. By 1866, the Freedmen's Bureau was operating 965 schools for 90,778 pupils.

# TO THE
# Freedmen.
## WENDELL PHILLIPS
## ON LEARNING TO READ AND WRITE.

BOSTON, July 16, 1865.

*My Dear Friend:*

You ask me what the North thinks about letting the Negro vote. My answer is, *two-thirds* of the North are willing he should vote, and *one* of these *thirds* is determined he *shall* vote, and will not rest till he does. But the opposition is very strong, and I fear we may see it put off for many a year.

Possibly there may be an agreement made, that those who can read and write shall vote, and no others.

Urge, therefore, every colored man *at once* to learn to read and write. His right to vote may very likely depend on that. Let him lose no time, but learn to read and write *at once*.

Yours truly,

Mr. JAMES REDPATH.        WENDELL PHILLIPS.

This public letter written by Wendell Phillips was part of the Republican drive to gain black suffrage. "No freedom is real," Phillips argued, "which does not place in the hands of the man himself the power to protect his own interests."

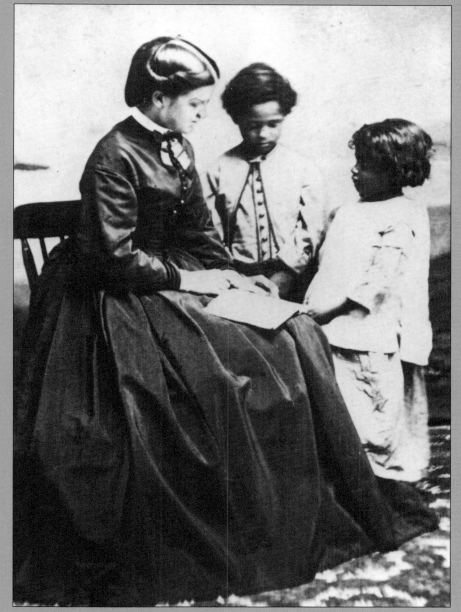

A Yankee schoolmarm helps her students in Beaufort, South Carolina in 1866. "The children were eager for knowledge," an official reported, "being stimulated by their parents, to whom knowledge of books had been like forbidden fruit."

## Educating a Generation of Leaders

The Freedmen's Bureau helped launch two dozen black colleges and universities, most of them church affiliated. "My strong wish was to lay permanent substructures as rapidly as possible," wrote Commissioner Oliver O. Howard, "in order to give good teachers, professional men and leaders to the rising generation of freedmen."

At first, the schools were institutions of higher learning in name only; for most of the poorly prepared students had yet to be taught the basics — reading, writing and arithmetic. Higher-level curricula were added later, chiefly in education, religion, and vocational and agricultural training.

Freedmen and women everywhere gave whatever they could to support the fledgling schools. In Jefferson City, Missouri, discharged soldiers contributed $6,325 to help in the founding of the Lincoln Institute. In Nashville, former slaves sold as scrap the rusting leg irons from the city's old slavepen to buy spelling books and Bibles for newly established Fisk University.

Visitors and students congregate outside the main building of Howard University in Washington, D.C., in 1870, the year that Howard graduated its first class of teachers. The university was named after former General Oliver O. Howard, who appropriated $30,000 from the Freedmen's Bureau budget to purchase land for the campus.

Hampton Institute's class of 1875 poses for a picture in front of Academic Hall in Hampton, Virginia. Standing at far left are General James F.B. Marshall, the school's treasurer, and General Samuel C. Armstrong, the principal. Seated in front of General Armstrong is chief teacher Mary Mackie. Booker T. Washington, who would become the class's most illustrious graduate, is in the front row, second from the left.

# The Radicals Ascendant

"I do not want to lose my faith in Andy Johnson," wrote New York lawyer and diarist George Templeton Strong in the winter of 1866. Strong's sentiment was shared by many others, but their confidence in the President was slipping nonetheless. Radical leader Wendell Phillips reflected the public mood in an impassioned speech called "The South Victorious." So extreme was Andrew Johnson's pro-Southern bias, thundered Phillips, that the South was winning in peace what it had lost in war. As for himself, said Phillips, he would rather have seen Grant surrender his sword to Lee than see Johnson cravenly submit to Southern politicians.

Phillips was a single-minded man of enormous energy, and his personal bias against the President was not shared by most critics of the Administration. But Johnson, with his inflexible opposition to any measure designed to improve the plight of Southern blacks, had managed to offend moderate as well as Radical Republicans. Suddenly his steadfast support for states' rights and his opposition to centralized government began to look less like loyalty to the Republic and more like sympathy for the South — and, worse, for the Democratic Party.

Increasingly alarmed, the Republican-dominated Joint Congressional Committee on Reconstruction labored throughout the winter and spring to hammer out its own program of reconstruction. In general, Radicals on the committee wanted to deny the right to vote to ex-Confederates, while giving it to Southern Negroes. Moderates thought that temporary disenfranchisement of the former Confederates would be sufficient punishment, and that it would do less damage to the Constitution to encourage (rather than require) the states to give the vote to blacks. The legislative program that emerged, admitted Senator James W. Grimes of Iowa, was "not exactly what any of us wanted, but we were each compelled to surrender some of our individual preferences in order to secure anything."

The compromise agreements were cast in the form of a constitutional amendment, the 14th, which was designed to make permanent the changes brought about by war and emancipation. Presented to Congress on April 30, 1866, and refined by weeks of heated debate, the Amendment consisted substantially of four sections. The first and most important provided a national definition of citizenship that embraced "all persons born or naturalized in the United States." The individual states were forbidden to abridge the rights of citizens or to deny them "the equal protection of the laws." Blacks were thus declared to be citizens and given a constitutional guarantee of their rights.

The second section gave further impetus to the enfranchisement of blacks. It declared that a state denying the vote to any adult male — except for untaxed Indians and "participants in the Rebellion" — would have its

President Andrew Johnson was fiercely proud of his plebeian origins; visiting author Charles Dickens said his face showed strength but lacked "genial sunlight."

representation in Congress reduced proportionally. The third section barred former Confederates from holding national or state office unless pardoned by Congress. The fourth section validated the national debt and repudiated the Confederate debt.

Adopted by both houses of Congress in June, the amendment was submitted for ratification to all the states — including those in the former Confederacy. Its reception in the South was predictably hostile. The Amendment was regarded as an intolerable assault on Southern theories of white supremacy because it would bar from office virtually the whole of the established ruling class — the men, as one landed Kentuckian put it, of "brains and property" and "civilized ancestry." For the South thus to renounce its leaders, many Southerners felt, would be to collaborate in its own destruction. "If we are to be degraded," wrote the Governor of North Carolina, "we will retain some self-esteem by not making it self-abasement."

The Amendment also ran into the implacable opposition of President Johnson, who considered it a rejection of his policies. In a message to Congress on the subject, he took a complex, legalistic position: The Congress could not amend the Constitution while unconstitutionally denying representation to some of the states.

The South, heartened by Johnson's sympathy, stiffened its opposition. Of the 11 Confederate states, only Tennessee, with its large Unionist following, ratified the Amendment and was readmitted at once.

As the most comprehensive statement of Republican aims, the 14th Amendment became the Party's platform in the congressional elections of 1866. Local issues aside, the elections were widely understood to be a referendum on Reconstruction. And President Johnson waded into the campaign fervently opposed to the Radicals who now controlled the majority party.

Johnson tried to forge a coalition of Democrats and conservative Republicans in support of his own program. The result was a new National Union Party, which held its convention in Philadelphia in August and endorsed the President's policy of immediate and unqualified readmission of the Southern states. In response, various Radical conventions were held in late summer, one of them involving veterans organizations, such as the Grand Army of the Republic, which were beginning to flex their political muscle. Elsewhere, Radical speakers compared Johnson to Judas Iscariot and Benedict Arnold.

Johnson damaged his public image when he embarked on an 18-day tour through the East and Middle West. Traveling by train, he stopped to declaim at one dusty crossroad after another in the first whistle-stop campaign ever undertaken by a President. Johnson attacked the 14th Amendment as illegal and defended himself as a martyr pilloried by a Radical Republican Congress and "a subsidized and mercenary press."

At some stops, Johnson was so severely heckled and even threatened that his train had to pull out of the station while he was still haranguing the crowd from the rear platform. Worse, he took to exchanging insults with the hecklers and engaging in shouting contests with the crowd. What should have been "a solemn journey," commented the New York *Tribune,* became instead "the stumping tour of an irritated demagogue." By the time Johnson got to St. Louis, he was babbling about Congressional attempts to remove him from office: "Yes, yes, they are

President Johnson sits between white-bearded Navy Secretary Gideon Welles and General Grant at an outdoor meal, during his futile 1866 campaign to promote leniency toward the South. A journalist covering the 18-day tour reported that Grant soon pronounced himself sick of it; "I am disgusted," he said, "at hearing a man make speeches on the way to his own funeral."

ready to impeach," he cried, to which a voice replied, "Too bad they don't."

In fact, talk of impeachment was much in the air after the President's disastrous "swing around the circle." The Republicans won a series of landslide victories that fall and achieved a majority of more than two thirds in both houses of Congress. It was clear that Johnson had lost his bid for popular support. An effort by the lameduck Congress to translate the impeachment talk into action failed in December, but a similar resolution in January of 1867 was referred to the Judiciary Committee of the House of Representatives for consideration.

Meantime, the voters of the 10 Southern states still not restored to the Union angrily refused to ratify the 14th Amendment. Thus denied the necessary approval of three fourths of the states, the Amendment was defeated — although in July of 1868 it would be declared to be in force by the questionable authority of a simple resolution endorsed by the House and Senate.

Radicals saw Southern rejection of the Amendment as declaring political war.

"They have deliberated, they have acted," cried Ohio Congressman James Garfield in February of 1867. "The last of the sinful ten has, with contempt and scorn, flung back into our teeth the magnanimous offer of a generous nation. It is now our turn to act."

Inflamed by Southern intransigence and invigorated by their electoral victories, the Republicans acted with a vengeance. On one momentous day — March 2, 1867 — Congress passed three acts over the President's veto that vastly reduced the power of the executive branch and imposed on the Southern states an entirely new set of conditions for their readmission to the Union. The first of the three, called the Reconstruction Act of 1867, eliminated the legal authority of existing Southern state governments, making them subservient to military rule, and spelled out the new requirements for readmission. While the Army ruled the 10 states that had refused to ratify the 14th Amendment, the civilians in each state would recast their system of government. This involved the registration of voters without regard to color; the election by these voters of delegates to a convention instructed to draft a new state constitution guaranteeing black suffrage; ratification of the resulting constitution and of the 14th Amendment to the federal Constitution; and the election under the transformed constitution of a new state government. Only then could a state be readmitted to the Union and regain its representation in Congress. Those former Confederates who were disqualified by the 14th Amendment from holding office also were barred from voting for convention delegates and from voting on the ratification of the new state constitutions.

Knowing that Johnson would try to frustrate the Reconstruction Act, Congress moved to limit his power. As part of an army appropriations bill enacted on March 2, it forbade the President to issue orders to the military governors, except through General in Chief Ulysses S. Grant. Congress also passed the Tenure of Office Act, forbidding the President to remove high-ranking civil officials, including Cabinet members, from his Administration without the consent of the Senate. This act was intended to protect Secretary of War Edwin Stanton, who vigorously supported Congress' reconstruction policy and was well placed to see it enforced.

In some of these actions, Congress was unabashedly exploring the limits of its constitutional authority. The legislative branch of the federal government had no established right, for example, to tell the states how to conduct their elections. The states had insisted at the Constitution's ratification that all those powers not specifically granted to the federal government were reserved to themselves. Moreover, in making ratification of the 14th Amendment a condition of readmission, Congress was subverting the clearly stipulated method for changing the Constitution, which required voluntary ratification by three fourths of the states.

But the Radicals were not going to let legal niceties stand in the way of punishing and transforming the unrepentant South. " 'Tis demanded by God and the spirit of the people," declared a pious Chicago Radical. Until the South had yielded "her idea of civilization" and allowed "the North to permeate her channels and to make her over," insisted Wendell Phillips, "reconstruction has not commenced." The editor and poet James Russell Lowell loftily told Southerners that

# A Confederate Hero at Peace

A few days after surrendering his army at Appomattox, Robert E. Lee rejoined his family in Richmond. Lee's situation was bleak: He was 58 years old and his 39-year military career was over. The family estate had been seized by the federal government, and Lee had no permanent home for his invalided wife, Mary Custis Lee, and their three daughters. He was bone-weary and his chest pained him, as it had since he suffered a mild heart attack in 1863.

Grieving for the Confederacy, uncertain how the authorities might punish him, Lee nevertheless vowed to be a force for reconciliation. "Go home," he told his Virginia veterans, "and help to build up the shattered fortunes of our old state." Then he proceeded to do his share (*following pages*).

Photographed by Mathew Brady a week after the surrender, Robert E. Lee still wears the three stars of a Confederate general on his collar. Standing beside him are his eldest son, Major General George Washington Custis Lee (*left*), and Lieutenant Colonel Walter H. Taylor, a longtime aide.

In a portrait that was made at Lee's request, the former general sits astride Traveller, his mount through most of the Civil War. Describing Traveller as "a Confederate grey," Lee commended the animal's "sagacity and affection."

Lee *(seated, second from left)* joins other dignitaries who have gathered to take the waters and renew social connections at White Sulphur Springs, West Virginia. Among the former Confederate generals present was P.G.T. Beauregard *(standing, fifth from left);* seated to the right of Lee are George Peabody and William Corcoran, Northern philanthropists who aided Washington College.

President Lee sits musing in his office in the basement of the Washington College chapel. Although he was a graduate and former superintendent of West Point, Lee minimized the regimentation of his students in Lexington, telling the faculty to "make no needless rules."

Lee and his wartime comrade Joseph Johnston (*left*) were both 63 when they met again in Savannah, in April of 1870, five years after surrendering the Confederacy's two largest armies. Their conversation was not recorded, but a local reporter noted on Lee's face a look of "inexpressible sadness."

# Rebuilding a Shattered College

The federal government charged Robert E. Lee with treason, and though he was never tried, neither was he pardoned. Wishing only to live quietly and write a history of the Army of Northern Virginia, he moved his family into a borrowed house west of Richmond. Then a trustee of Washington College in Lexington, Virginia, made him an unexpected offer: Would Lee serve as president of that nearly defunct school?

Lee said yes, and tackled the new career with vigor. He saw it as a chance "to aid in the restoration of peace and harmony." With funds from donors nationwide, he hired faculty, erected buildings, restocked the library and planted trees. Perhaps most vital to the future of the South was the curriculum he installed, which replaced some classical studies with departments of chemistry, law and engineering.

With the ceaseless work, however, came renewed chest pains. The family's 1869 visit to a West Virginia spa was as much for Lee's benefit as for his wife's.

# Last Honors for a Revered Commander

Lee's heart condition — he called it rheumatism — increasingly hindered him in the late 1860s. His rides on Traveller became less frequent, and though he continued to collect material for his memoirs, he never began writing them.

On September 28, 1870, at supper, Lee suffered a stroke. Students, faculty and family grieved as he lay nearly mute, fancying himself on old battlefields. He died on October 11, his last words the familiar command: "Strike the tent."

In memory of the general and his achievement in revitalizing Washington College, the trustees — a mere two weeks after his death — agreed to change the name of the school to Washington and Lee University.

Mourners crowd around the Washington College chapel for Lee's funeral; Washington Hall (*left*) and other campus buildings are hung with crepe.

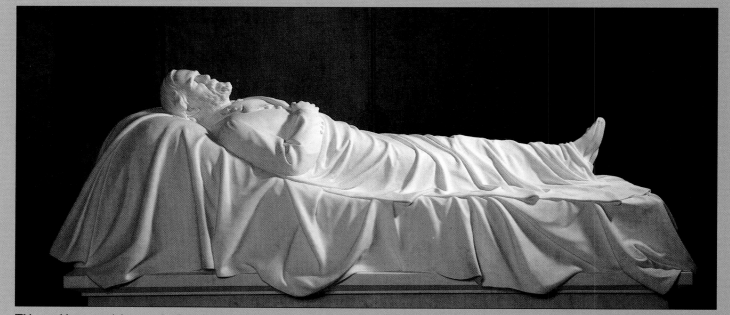

This marble memorial, near the Lee family crypt at Washington and Lee University, depicts General Lee asleep in his Confederate uniform.

Northerners were prepared to give them lessons in citizenship and "by God's grace, to Americanize" them.

Aside from these missionary-like impulses, many Radicals had very practical reasons for wanting to regenerate the South. Historically, Southern and Western agrarian interests had outvoted the conservative business groups of the industrial Northeast. Only after the departure of Southern senators in 1861 had the industrialists been able to obtain passage of high, protective tariffs. Most Northeastern manufacturers did not want Southerners back in Congress until they were sure the Southerners would support a strong tariff — or, as former New York Governor Horatio Seymour sarcastically put it, "until their ideas of business, industry, money making, spindles and looms were in accord with those of Massachusetts."

To all of these Northern expressions of intent, sacred and profane, the South reacted with bitterness and apprehension. Rather than Reconstruction, wrote Elizabeth Meriwether of Kentucky, the Radical program "more properly should be called 'Destruction.' " "Oh, my God," cried Emma Holmes of South Carolina in her diary, "when will the dark days end which seem enveloping our stricken land in deeper gloom, day by day." Holmes gave Johnson credit for "struggling against the ferocious Black Republicans for the rights of the South and the white man"; but even so, she noted, "an almost unlimited military despotism is holding the South as conquered territory" and "despair is laying its icy hand on all."

In practice, the military rule set up by the Reconstruction Act was rarely despotic and it lacked the force to lay an icy hand on anything like the whole of Southern society. In the first years of military occupation, about 200,000 soldiers were stationed in the entire South. The garrisons at Richmond and New Orleans had 1,000 men each, and no other post had more than 500. Many military commanders doubted their ability to maintain order even in the limited areas where their troops were concentrated.

The 10 recalcitrant Southern states were placed in five military districts, each administered by a brigadier or major general. These officers varied greatly in their political allegiance. On the advice of General Grant, the President on March 11, 1867, appointed John M. Schofield as commander in the first district (Virginia); Daniel E. Sickles in the second (North and South Carolina); John Pope in the third (Georgia, Alabama and Florida); Edward O. C. Ord in the fourth (Mississippi and Arkansas); and Philip H. Sheridan in the fifth (Louisiana and Texas).

What was notable about this first list of appointments (which would change many times in the months to come) was that all the appointees supported Congressional rather than presidential reconstruction. Johnson's reason for being so conciliatory toward his opponents was that the House Judiciary Committee still was inquiring into his conduct, seeking grounds for impeachment.

On March 23, Congress passed a second Reconstruction Act that required the district commanders to register eligible voters, including the freed slaves, and to set the machinery in motion for the election of delegates to constitutional conventions. Regardless of their personal biases, most of the generals tried to administer the Reconstruction Acts, as Sheridan put it, "without fear or favor." It was not a simple task. The military and civilian authorities in Washing-

ton preferred to leave the difficult, confrontational decisions to the commanders in the field. "You will use the troops of your command to preserve order without referring to these headquarters," read a typical directive.

On the other hand, the generals were often harassed about their decisions after they made them. Within a few months, President Johnson began criticizing generals he thought were assuming too authoritarian a role. In June he had the U.S. Attorney General define the Army's function as being confined to simple police duty. Military commanders were not to remove civilian officials, and their registrars had to accept without question a prospective voter's oath that he had not served the Confederacy.

Grant promptly told his generals that this ruling did not have the force of an order, and Congress, overriding a veto by Johnson, passed a supplementary measure nullifying it. But military commanders would continue to be caught in a political crossfire as long as the Army remained in the South.

The generals approached the forbidding job of maintaining order — while avoiding bloodshed — in a variety of ways. Some commanders banned parades, suppressed historical societies and forbade Confederate veterans to form organized groups. Others continued to remove civil officials who displeased them as "impediments to Reconstruction." All told, the governors of five states and thousands of local officials, down

A Federal regiment assembles for a dress parade outside its Memphis barracks in June of 1865. Federal troops continued to garrison many Southern cities after the War, as military governments supplanted the civil governments of the Confederacy.

to cemetery sextons, were thus removed from office. Military courts for the most part took precedence over civilian ones, although some district commanders were more circumspect than others about intervening in purely civil offenses and disputes.

Despite their generally light-handed approach, the district commanders were regarded by Southern whites as "military satraps," "viceroys" and "despots." Sheridan was particularly disliked in Louisiana, where he adhered to the letter of the Reconstruction Acts: forcibly registering black voters, disenfranchising ex-Confederates and removing scores of state and city officials. Sickles, who had lost a leg at Gettysburg, was hated in North and South Carolina. On the other hand, Major General Lovell Rousseau, who was one of Sheridan's successors in Louisiana, so endeared himself to whites by his almost total inaction that when he died unexpectedly on duty, he was afforded one of the largest funeral processions ever seen in New Orleans. The Alexandria *Democrat* hailed him as having "respected the feelings and even the prejudices of our people."

Most disturbing to Southern prejudices were the efforts of the military governments to ensure the registration of black voters. Many Southerners saw such efforts as part of a Northern plot to give blacks political dominance over their former masters. Although whites outnumbered blacks three to two in most of the South, the disqualification of former Confederates brought the two races closer to parity in potential voting power.

The Reconstruction Acts in effect reduced Southern voters to three groups — blacks, Northerners who had resided in the South for at least one year, and white Southerners who had not held Confederate office and who could prove their loyalty to the Union. Northerners who had moved to the South were commonly referred to as "carpetbaggers" — a word derived from their supposed practice of bringing with them their worldly possessions, crammed into a cheap carpetbag. Southern Unionists were called "scalawags" — a term that can be traced to the town of Scalloway in the Shetland Islands, known for its scrubby cattle. It signified something runty, mean, scabby or venomous. Both terms were highly charged emotionally and had an important influence on attitudes in both North and South.

Horace Greeley, the outspoken editor of the New York *Tribune,* characterized carpetbaggers as individuals intent on "stealing and plundering, many of them with both arms around Negroes, and their hands in their rear pockets, seeing if they cannot pick a paltry dollar out of them." Similarly, an Alabama commentator saw the scalawag as "a mangy dog, slinking through the alleys — defiling with tobacco juice the steps of the Capitol, stretching his lazy carcass in the sun on the Square." Both carpetbaggers and scalawags were thought to be growing fat on loot plundered from the prostrate South.

The reality was considerably different. Although there certainly were opportunists among the carpetbaggers, there were also many idealists who wanted to regenerate the South, improve its economy, and encourage understanding and tolerance between the races. Many Northerners went South as teachers, clergymen, officers of the Freedmen's Bureau or agents of the various benevolent societies engaged in distributing aid to blacks. They were a highly educated group — nearly two thirds of the carpetbaggers who eventually were elected to state legislatures practiced a profession — and they often took considerable capital with them when they went south.

A large percentage of the immigrants were Union Army veterans who had served in the South, admired the region and were eager to get back there. By the autumn of 1866, well over 20,000 ex-Union soldiers had settled in the South, more than 5,000 of them in Louisiana alone. Many of these Union veterans were well received by the people they had so recently fought. Among those who prospered was Colonel John T. Wilder, famed during the fighting in Tennessee as the organizer and leader of Wilder's Lightning Brigade of Indiana. Wilder purchased large tracts of land rich in iron and coal near Knoxville, Tennessee, and built up extensive interests in mining, cement, cotton and banking. He became so popular that eventually a military training camp outside Knoxville was named after him.

Equally popular was Lieutenant B. H. True of the 136th New York Volunteers, who began farming in Georgia in 1865, with such success that he launched a newspaper and was elected to the state agricultural society as the "celebrated farmer from Morgan County." Both Wilder and True saw the South as a new frontier — as did Captain Clinton A. Cilley of New Hampshire, who had served in Sherman's drive through North Carolina in 1865 and returned there the following year to practice law. Cilley eventually became a judge of the superior court and was cited as "one of North Carolina's ablest lawyers and finest citizens."

More in keeping with the popular image of the carpetbagger was a colonel from Illinois named Milton S. Littlefield, who had studied law in Abraham Lincoln's Springfield office. Littlefield moved to North Carolina in 1867 and made a fortune as a speculator in state bonds and as a lobbyist for the railroad interests. Although Littlefield came to be known as the "Prince of Carpetbaggers," he could not have succeeded without the collaboration of native North Carolinians, most notably Governor William W. Holden. Littlefield left the state toward the end of the Reconstruction era and resisted efforts to extradite him to stand trial on charges of bribery and embezzlement. The efforts were dropped after he showed a visiting North Carolina official certain papers indicating who his collaborators had been. "Colonel, I respect your condition," said the official. "I do not think we will trouble you any more."

The depredations of men such as Littlefield angered the South less than the political activities of the Northern reformers. One of the most celebrated and least popular of these was a former lieutenant colonel of the 2nd Wisconsin Volunteers named Albert T. Morgan. Aflame with the vision of bringing racial justice to the South, Morgan moved to Mississippi in 1865. In the xenophobic environs of Yazoo City, he soon made himself suspect by criticizing local race relations and openly consorting with blacks. After trying without success to grow cotton on a leased plantation, Morgan was elected state senator and then sheriff with the combined support of whites and blacks. Resentment of Morgan ran so deep, however, that the incumbent sheriff refused to leave office and was shot down in a gun battle with Morgan's followers. The new sheriff was honest and dedicated, but he alienated local residents by marrying a beautiful quadroon schoolteacher from New York. A posse of whites

Inexpensive suitcases made from carpeting, such as the one above, inspired the epithet "carpetbaggers" for Northerners who thronged to the South after the War ended. One well-intentioned Ohioan who traveled to North Carolina later remarked ruefully: "We tried to superimpose the idea of civilization, the idea of the North, upon the South at a moment's warning. It was a fool's errand."

eventually came for Morgan — "with ropes over the pommels of their saddles, and pistols and knives in the belts," he recalled — and he had to flee the county in disguise.

Most carpetbaggers took an interest in the politics of the South because they were anxious to protect their investment in the region by encouraging stable economic growth. They gravitated to the Republican Party both out of sympathy for its goals and out of a conviction that the Democrats were too disoriented and obstructionist to be effective. Carpetbaggers played an important role in the Congressionally mandated state conventions of 1867 and 1868, comprising in most states between one quarter and one half of the delegates. But an even more important part was played by the detested scalawags.

As was true of the carpetbaggers, the scalawags were maligned unfairly; they rarely conformed to the stereotypical "scaly, scabby runts" of popular mythology. Some of the scalawags were indeed poor upland whites who bitterly resented both the blacks and the planters — "Let the slave-holding aristocracy no longer rule you," read a Republican handbill of 1868 addressed to the "Poor White Men of Georgia." But it was also true that many planters and businessmen were included in the scalawag ranks.

These men were simply being practical. They were confident that they could control the black vote, and the Republican Party seemed to them to be the party of modernization, through which they could work for Southern commercial and industrial development and a reduction in the tax burden. "Yankees and Yankee notions are just what we want," proclaimed one enthusiastic scalawag. "We want their capital to build factories and workshops and railroads. We want their energy and enterprise to operate these factories, and to teach us how to do it."

James L. Alcorn, a wealthy planter who became the first Republican governor of Mississippi, went even further. Alcorn was no Radical: He opposed legislation to enforce social equality between the races and he worked to bring former Confederates back into government. But on the issue of voting rights he proposed not only to vote with the Negro, he said, but "to discuss political affairs with him; to sit, if need be, in political counsel with him; and from a platform acceptable alike to him, to me, and to you, to pluck our common liberty and our common prosperity out of the jaws of inevitable ruin." Such statements were anathema to most Southerners. Having "dishonored the dignity of white blood," said an angry Democrat, scalawags such as Alcorn stood revealed as "the vilest renegades of the South, traitors alike to principle and race."

Yet the scalawags included some Confederate heroes. Perhaps the most celebrated, and resented, was Lieutenant General James A. Longstreet, who moved to New Orleans after the War to become a cotton broker and president of an insurance firm. Accepting the "arbitrament of the sword," Longstreet argued that the South's only option was to work with the victors. In 1867, he joined the Republican Party and endorsed the Radicals' plan of Reconstruction.

While such men were sincere in their political convictions, other scalawags became Republicans purely for personal gain. Perhaps the most notorious was Colonel Franklin J. Moses Jr. of South Carolina, an ardent secessionist who in 1861 had raised the Confederate flag over Fort Sumter. Moses hastened to join the Republicans after the War, won the governorship of his state — and systematically looted the public treasury.

Moses' record was equaled by Governor Joseph Brown of Georgia. A passionate advocate of states' rights and a Democrat, Brown had no apparent difficulty joining the Republicans during Radical Reconstruction and urging Southern adoption of the Radicals' terms. He returned to the Democrats as soon as Republican rule was overthrown and made a fortune in iron and coal mining, Atlanta real estate and railroading. In his later years, this agile onetime scalawag virtually ruled Georgia as the state's undisputed Democratic boss and as its Democratic senator in Washington.

The Republican Party that was thrust toward power in the South by the Reconstruction Acts of 1867 was thus a frail coalition of apparently irreconcilable parts — blacks and whites, Northerners and Southerners, idealists and opportunists, educated and uneducated, rich and poor. The so-called crackers who dreamed of occupying the lands of the planters — who constantly asked, a Union officer recalled, "When is our folks a-gwine

Hat in hand, a former slave is shown casting his first ballot in this 1867 engraving, which appeared in *Frank Leslie's Illustrated Newspaper*. The Northern publication lauded the new voters for their "good sense, discretion, and modesty."

to git the lan'?" — seemed to have nothing in common with the aristocrats they detested. Yet for a time the unlikely Republican alliance not only survived, but thrived.

In Radical eyes, the key figure in that alliance was the black voter. During the screening and registering of voters, Army commanders had to continually guard against white attempts to intimidate blacks and keep them from the polls. So inflamed was white opinion, noted the deposed governor of South Carolina, that he anticipated a "terrific war of extermination" against the former slaves. Bands of armed whites gathered at black churches and other registration points, and employers threatened freedmen with dismissal if they exercised their right to vote.

Many illiterate blacks had no idea what

registration was. When called to the polls, noted a correspondent for the New York *Herald*, they sometimes "brought along bags and baskets 'to put it in,' and in nearly every instance there was a great rush for fear we would not have 'enough to go around.' Quite a few thought it was the distribution of confiscated lands under a new name."

Under the circumstances, it was remarkable that blacks became part of the electoral process at all. Much of the credit went to two agencies — the Union League and the Freedmen's Bureau. Founded in Philadelphia during the War as an anti-Copperhead organization, the Union League developed into a powerful political branch of the radical wing of the Republican Party. To encourage black voters, the league organized secret lodges, with elaborate initiation ceremonies and Masonic-like rituals. Bureau agents worked closely with the league to promote Republican candidates among the former slaves.

Democrats made their own efforts to woo blacks — by inviting them to fish fries and barbecues and by reminding them of the care they had been given when they were slaves. Not surprisingly, the Democrats failed almost totally. They then accused the Union League of voting the freedmen like "herds of senseless cattle." There was evidence to support the charge: A reporter observed agents of the league lining up blacks and marching them past the ballot boxes to vote "once for me, once for Jim who couldn't come." But in fact, the Democrats' insistence on white supremacy made black allegiance to the Republican Party almost inevitable.

When the registration of voters in the 10 unreconstructed Southern states was completed in September of 1867, there were an estimated 735,000 blacks and 635,000 whites on the rolls. Some Democratic leaders urged their followers not to vote in the subsequent elections, on the ground that if a majority of the registered voters did not go to the polls, any vote in favor of holding a constitutional convention would be invalid. Nevertheless, in every state the proconvention vote exceeded the necessary majority, and the Republicans won resounding victories.

The conventions that followed were derided by the Democratic press as "Bones and Banjo Conventions," and some newspapers put the word "nigger" after the name of every black delegate. In fact, blacks constituted a majority of delegates in only one state — South Carolina — and leadership at the conventions was largely in the hands of white carpetbaggers, who exercised an influence out of proportion to their numbers.

The constitutions that emerged from the conventions were the most enlightened the South had ever known and far more compassionate than many constitutions in the North. They established universal male suffrage and gave the South its first system of universal public education. Several obligated the states to care for the disadvantaged — the insane, the orphaned, the poor, the deaf and dumb. Some eliminated imprisonment for debt and reformed local government and judicial administration. They protected homesteads from foreclosure and supported industrialization and immigration. They removed property qualifications for voting and holding office, thus depriving the planter class of its monopoly on political power.

White Southerners tried to prevent ratification of the new constitutions by intimidation and by boycotting the polls so that the required majority of registered voters could not be mustered in their favor. After this

tactic worked in Alabama, Congress quickly acted to eliminate the majority requirement. Seven states — Alabama, Arkansas, Florida, Georgia, Louisiana, North Carolina and South Carolina — then ratified their respective constitutions. They installed Republican governments and after ratification of the 14th Amendment were received back into the Union in June of 1868. In Georgia, however, military rule was temporarily revived when the legislature expelled its new black members. After reseating them, Georgia was readmitted to the Union in 1870 along with Texas, Virginia and Mississippi.

Legally, Reconstruction appeared to be complete; in truth, it had barely begun. Far from diminishing, Southern intransigence increased after the Reconstruction governments came to power. The fury of Southerners was directed mostly at blacks in public office — even though former slaves were not represented in proportion to their numbers and were rarely in a majority in any branch of government. Blacks outnumbered whites, intermittently, only in the legislature of South Carolina, and no black was ever governor of a reconstructed state. The majority of black officeholders were local officials such as justices of the peace and county superintendents of education, but even there they did not hold a proportionate share of offices.

On the national level, only two blacks sat in the United States Senate and 15 in the House of Representatives during the whole of the Reconstruction period. Although black votes sustained the Republican machines in the South, many white Republicans, whether of the North or South, privately shared the Democrats' belief that blacks were not competent to govern.

Those blacks who did come to office performed about as well — and as badly — as whites. They were honest and dishonest, intelligent and stupid, industrious and lazy. For example, there was Pinckney Benton Stewart Pinchback, who was said to be the son of a Mississippi planter and a slave woman. After being emancipated by his father and sent to school in Ohio, Pinchback had enlisted in the Union Army and for a time he had commanded a company of colored troops in the Corps d'Afrique. Settling in Louisiana, he became lieutenant governor in the state's corrupt postwar government. His idea of reconstruction seemed to be largely self-enrichment, and he quickly became a very wealthy man.

Far more responsible were the two black U.S. Senators from Mississippi — Hiram Rhodes Revels and Blanche K. Bruce — who fought for honest state government regardless of party. Revels, born a free black and educated at Knox College in Illinois, dared to turn against the graft-ridden local Republican Party to which he owed his political career. Bruce, born a slave, had the vision to fight for Indian rights and against the policy of Chinese exclusion. Both men worked not only for the rights of blacks, but for better white-black relations and for an end to discrimination against former Confederates.

In most instances, the blacks who served in government were the elite of their race. Of those elected to state or federal office, about 80 percent were literate and 25 percent had been free before the War. A sizable percentage were from the North. Most were either professionals — clergymen predominated — artisans, small businessmen or independent farmers. A few had exceptional educational backgrounds. Florida's Secretary of State, Jonathan Gibbs, had degrees from Dart-

A mobile brass band pauses on a street in Baton Rouge to drum up support for a Republican candidate for the Louisiana State Senate. The prominent role of Northerners and Union loyalists in the campaign is evident from the prominent display of Federal regimental colors at right.

**69**

mouth College and the Princeton Theological Seminary; South Carolina's Secretary of State and subsequent Treasurer, Francis L. Cardozo, had trained at the University of Glasgow and at St. Andrews Theological Seminary in Scotland. Robert Brown Elliott, South Carolina's second black U.S. Congressman, had attended Eton College in England and spoke several languages well. More important for his political career, Elliott had a knowledge of the law. Once he addressed a hostile white audience on the Constitution. He began by placing a copy of the Constitution on the lectern with a Colt revolver on either side of it, explaining coolly that he was prepared to defend his speech.

The attitude of these men and other black legislators was not vindictive. One black politician in Alabama noted that he had no desire "to take away any rights of the white man: All I want is equal rights in the Court House and equal rights when I go to vote." Nevertheless, the excesses of the Reconstruction governments were invariably blamed on their black members, even though power in Southern states remained largely in white control. The theme of the "barbarous African" dominating and "overwhelming civilization" quickly became a staple of Democratic propaganda. In Alabama, Democrats observed the day on which the predominantly white Reconstruction government came to power by calling for fasting and prayer for the deliverance of the state "from the horrors of Negro domination."

Unable to block the establishment of the Reconstruction governments, President Johnson did what he could to weaken the effect of the legislation that brought them into being. He plotted to get rid of Secretary of War Stanton, who had become increasingly vocal in his support of the South's Radical program. Because the Tenure of Office Act forbade him from removing Stanton without Senate approval, Johnson took a devious course. He waited until the Senate had adjourned for the summer of 1867. Then, on August 12, he suspended Stanton and prevailed on General Grant to take over the War Office until the Senate reconvened.

To further impede his Congressional opponents, Johnson removed the military district officers who were vigorously enforcing the Reconstruction Acts. He had soon replaced all but one of them with generals more sympathetic to the South. Sheridan and Sickles were dismissed in August, Pope and Ord in December. For good measure, Johnson replaced some Radical-leaning officials of the Freedmen's Bureau, most notably Major General Wager Swayne in Alabama.

Though Democrats applauded the moves, most reaction in the North was hostile. Some dismissed generals became overnight heroes: When Sheridan visited St. Louis, for example, 30,000 people turned out in a procession two miles long to honor him and to express displeasure with the President.

Yet results of the state elections in the fall of 1867 indicated that many Northerners shared some of Johnson's attitudes, particularly his opposition to black advancement. Republicans, having enfranchised Southern blacks, felt compelled to do the same for those in the North. Democrats, however, played on Northern racial fears. Visiting French journalist and future premier Georges Clemenceau noted dryly that "any Democrat who did not manage to hint in his speech that the Negro is a degenerate gorilla, would be considered lacking in enthusi-

Hiram R. Revels (*top*) and Blanche K. Bruce (*bottom*) were the two blacks elected to the United States Senate during Reconstruction. Both represented Mississippi: Revels, a Methodist minister, held Jefferson Davis' former seat in 1870 and 1871 and Bruce, a former school superintendent, served from 1875 to 1881.

A broadside commemorating the new Louisiana constitution, rewritten under the 1867 Reconstruction Acts, salutes the most prominent of the 48 black convention delegates, many of whom also became state legislators. Oscar J. Dunn (*center*) and Pinckney B. S. Pinchback (*bottom*) were two of the three blacks to serve Louisiana as lieutenant governor during Reconstruction.

asm." In Ohio, girls dressed in white paraded through the streets with banners reading, "Fathers, save us from Negro equality."

In the end, fear prevailed: Voters in Ohio, Minnesota and Kansas rejected black suffrage outright. Elsewhere, Democrats made major gains. One of Johnson's aides explained the Republican defeat by remarking that "any party with an abolition head and a nigger tail will soon find itself with nothing left but the head and the tail." Johnson himself gave a victory speech in which he claimed vindication by the people.

In fact, Johnson's elation was premature. Although a second attempt to impeach him was defeated by a margin of 2 to 1 in the House early in December, Johnson further antagonized Congress by asking for a special vote of thanks to Major General Winfield Scott Hancock, a Democrat who had taken Sheridan's place as commander of the Louisiana-Texas district. As Hancock had just declared the supremacy of civil over military government, in direct repudiation of the Reconstruction Acts, Johnson's request was an affront to Radical Republicans.

As a result, the Senate was in a belligerent mood when it met after the Christmas holidays and refused to endorse the suspension of Stanton. Grant moved out of the office of the Secretary of War, and Stanton moved back in. Johnson accused Grant of disloyalty, and their angry exchange of letters made front-page copy in the press.

Johnson now took the rash step of dismissing Stanton outright, in defiance of the Tenure of Office Act, and replacing him with Adjutant General Lorenzo Thomas. There followed a comic-opera sequence in which Thomas tried to assume his new job, only to find Stanton barricaded in his office. While the two men debated who was the true Secretary of War, Congress again took steps to remove Johnson, whom his Republican opponents were calling "The Great Obstruction." On February 24, 1868, Representative John Covode of Pennsylvania offered a resolution that Johnson "be impeached of high crimes and misdemeanors."

The House quickly passed the resolution by a party-line vote of 126 to 47 and appointed a committee to "report articles of impeachment." In so doing, the legislators were ignoring the constitutional impeachment procedure, which called for an investigation first and then, if warranted, the drawing up of formal charges. Johnson was, in effect, presumed guilty before he was tried.

The committee included some of the most radical men in Congress — most notably Thaddeus Stevens of Pennsylvania. In emotionally heated Washington, Johnson had been accused of everything from adultery and alcoholism to conspiring with John Wilkes Booth to murder Lincoln. Responsible men hardly heeded such charges, but there was a real concern that the President was leading the country toward another civil war. A rumor spread that Johnson intended to storm the War Department with Marines and force Stanton from office; a Radical senator and a congressman mounted guard with a hundred men, and the local garrison commander placed his officers on alert. "What does Johnson mean to do?" asked a former attorney general. "Does he mean to have another rebellion?"

Some of Johnson's enemies suggested that merely obstructing the will of the majority party constituted grounds for removal: Johnson had vetoed 20 bills in three years, thus surpassing the previous record of 11 ve-

Of the seven congressmen (*above*) named to manage the 1868 impeachment of Andrew Johnson, Thaddeus Stevens (*with cane*) and Benjamin Butler (*far left*) were the most zealous. Stevens had led an earlier drive to remove Johnson from office; Butler, an experienced trial lawyer, prepared the House's opening statement and presented it to the Senate "in the same manner," he said, as he would try a horse thief.

toes in eight years set a generation earlier by Andrew Jackson. In the end, the House framed and presented to the Senate — constitutionally responsible for hearing impeachment proceedings — a list of 11 charges. They focused on Johnson's plot to remove Stanton in violation of the Tenure of Office Act. The first nine articles all dealt with this theme, the 10th invoked Johnson's "inflammatory and scandalous harangues," against the Congress, and the 11th was a relentless summary of all the accusations. But the basic — unspecified — accusation was that the President had obstructed Republican Reconstruction and favored the South.

When the trial began in March of 1868, the seven managers named by the House to present the charges to the Senate so overstated their case that a reaction of sympathy for the President soon set in. The most energetic and histrionic of the managers was former General Benjamin Butler of Massachusetts. In a spirited address, Butler tried to demonstrate how desperate the situation in the South had become under Johnson; he waved a nightshirt allegedly stained by the blood of an Ohio carpetbagger who had been flogged by racist ruffians in Mississippi.

President Johnson's attorneys mounted a purely legal defense emphasizing the fragile nature of the case. Was it a crime worthy of impeachment, asked Boston-born lawyer William M. Evarts, for a President to remove a member of his own Cabinet? As the trial progressed, even the anti-Johnson magazine *The Nation* conceded that "the Managers were overmastered throughout in learning and ability."

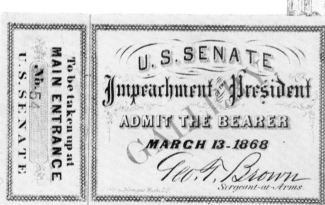

U. S. SENATE

Impeachment of President

ADMIT THE BEARER

MARCH 13 - 1868

Geo. T. Brown
*Sergeant-at-Arms.*

To be taken up at
MAIN ENTRANCE

No. 54

U. S. SENATE

U. S. SENATE

This ticket, signed by the Senate's sergeant-at-arms, admitted the bearer to the impeachment trial. Five policemen were needed to control the crowds.

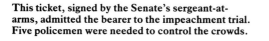

A Senate clerk's tally sheet records the votes taken on three of the 11 articles of impeachment brought against Johnson. Falling one vote short of the required two-thirds majority on each of these charges, Johnson's accusers conceded defeat.

The galleries teem with spectators, and the aisles are crowded with visiting members of the House, as the Senate chamber becomes a courtroom for the trial of Andrew Johnson. In this engraving, one of Johnson's lawyers (*foreground*) rises to address the bench, where Chief Justice Salmon Chase presides; the impeachment managers sit at the far table, with Benjamin Butler at their front. Butler wanted Johnson summoned and made to stand "until the Senate offered him a chair." But the President was not obligated to attend.

The trial dragged on for eight weeks, and passions cooled. Many moderate senators unsympathetic to Johnson began to fear that if he were removed, the presidency would be compromised and the constitutional balance of powers destroyed. Johnson conducted himself with restraint throughout, giving signs of enforcing the Reconstruction Acts and appointing a widely respected moderate, General John Schofield, to occupy the disputed office of Secretary of War. These ac-

tions helped swing seven moderate Republican senators to his side. Maine Senator William P. Fessenden spoke for all of them, saying he could vote against Johnson if he "were impeached for general cussedness," but "that is not the question to be tried."

The seven votes were recognized as crucial. Johnson needed 19 votes to survive in office, and he could count on only the Senate's nine Democrats and three conservative Republicans to cast their ballots against impeachment. Enormous Republican pressure was brought to bear on the wavering senators to bring them back into line. Bishop Matthew Simpson, called on to use his influence to see that his fellow Methodist, Senator Waitman T. Willey of West Virginia, was "saved from error," got a church conference to set aside an hour of prayer for the President's conviction. The Radical-dominated Tennessee legislature passed a resolution demanding that Tennessee Senator Joseph O. Fowler vote for impeachment. Denounced by some of his constituents as "a traitor and a Judas" for leaning toward the President, Iowa Senator James W. Grimes suffered a mild stroke. But the "Treacherous Seven," as the infuriated Radicals called them, would not vote to convict the President. The final tally was 35 for conviction and 19 against, one vote short of the necessary two-thirds majority. Johnson was acquitted.

By this time, the public had grown weary of the trial and was already caught up in the presidential campaign of 1868. Even as the impeachment vote had been going on, the Republican Party had gathered in Chicago to nominate its candidate. There was little doubt in anybody's mind who that would be — General Ulysses S. Grant.

# A Wild Rush for Riches

*"After our rebellion, when so many young men were at liberty to return to their homes, they found they were not satisfied with the farm, the store, or the work-shop of the villages. The war begot a spirit of independence and enterprise."*

ULYSSES S. GRANT, *PERSONAL MEMOIRS*

The ascension of Ulysses S. Grant to the presidency of the United States was a paradoxical affair. Grant did not seek the Republican nomination in 1868; he even told his friend William Tecumseh Sherman that he would avoid it, if he could. (It would be 16 years before Sherman would demonstrate the surest method for declining a presidential nomination, with his famous message to the Republican convention of 1884: "I will not accept if nominated and will not serve if elected.") Yet the reluctant Grant was nominated unanimously on the first ballot at the party's May gathering in Chicago.

"Let us have peace," Grant urged the divided party he had been chosen to lead. It was his destiny, however, to endure one of the most contentious and violent campaigns in the nation's history. The Democrats, who spurned the incumbent Andrew Johnson and nominated former New York Governor Horatio Seymour, accused the Republican Congress of imposing "military despotism" on the South. They insisted that the Reconstruction Acts were "unconstitutional, revolutionary and void." In the South, white supremacists launched a campaign of terror designed to prevent blacks and their supporters from voting. "I intend to kill Radicals," vowed the Ku Klux Klan's General Nathan Bedford Forrest; subsequently, more than 200 political murders were reported in Arkansas alone.

Republicans reminded voters that Sey-

mour had not served in the War and that the Democratic Party had been the party of secession. "Scratch a Democrat," went the Republican campaign slogan, "and you find a rebel under his skin." In the North these charges, along with reaction to the widespread violence in the South, hurt the Democrats. But there was also a heavy backlash against Republicans from Northerners who were beginning to realize that Republicans meant to enfranchise blacks in the North.

In the end, Grant was elected. He won 214 electoral votes to Seymour's 80, but his margin in the popular vote was far more modest — 300,000 votes out of 5.7 million cast. Grant had been given this majority by the blacks; just three years after the end of the War, most white voters had favored the Democrats — the party of rebellion.

Instead of the peace he espoused, President Grant would find himself and the country enmeshed in violence — a dark tide of mayhem and murder that would threaten to plunge the country again into civil war. Grant was the general who had won the War, and he represented stubborn, uncompromising effectiveness; yet his Administration would be marked from the beginning by the incompetence of his subordinates. He was the embodiment of flinty, Western probity, yet scandal would taint the doings of the federal government virtually from the moment he took its reins. The hard-driving, self-confident general would be transformed in-

A hatless Ulysses S. Grant rides with a galaxy of Union Army generals in this idealized painting honoring the Civil War's conquering heroes. Although Grant had no experience or particular interest in politics, his towering reputation as an unflappable military leader earned him the Republican Party's unanimous nomination for President in 1868.

to an uncertain, confused president. Nor would he be the only one to lose his way in the bewildering new era into which the triumphant North led a nation still divided.

On a hot July night in 1868, not long after the nomination of Grant, the scion of a distinguished American family returned to Boston after seven years abroad. The young man, Henry Adams, had spent the war years as a private secretary to his father, U.S. Ambassador to England Charles Francis Adams.

As a thunderstorm lashed Boston Harbor that night, Henry Adams recalled, the family "clambered down the side of their Cunard steamer into the government tugboat, which set them ashore in black darkness at the end of some North River pier. Had they been Tyrian traders of the year B.C. 1000, landing from a galley fresh from Gibraltar, they could hardly have been stranger on the shore of a world so changed from what it had been ten years before."

The sense of strangeness that afflicted Henry Adams on that North River pier reflected the bewilderment of the old establishment confronted with the new. Adams was the descendant of two presidents and "Heaven knew how many Puritans and Patriots";

yet his illustrious heritage counted for little before the "great mechanical energies" of the new America. Adams and his kind were as estranged from their country, he felt, as were the fast-disappearing Indians and buffalo of the Great Plains.

Although few Americans shared Henry Adams' pride of lineage, many sensed as he did that their lives in the postwar era would never again be the same. The enormous economic innovations that Adams feared were not the only forces working for change. The West was opening, and the United States was transforming into a continental power. There was the shift of Eastern population toward the cities, the flood of foreign immigration, the "rough overturning of old social ranks," in the words of the writer Bayard Taylor, and the emergence of "barbaric wealth" and a newly affluent middle class. All of these phenomena engaged the energies and attention of most Americans far more than the reconstruction of the nation.

They were trends that had existed before the War and had been accelerated by it. When Abraham Lincoln took office as president, observed Senator John Sherman of Ohio, he had been expected "to protect by wise revenue laws, the labor of our people; to secure the public lands to actual settlers; to develop the internal resources of the country by opening new means of communication between the Atlantic and the Pacfic."

These were familiar Republican ambitions that had been blocked in the past by Southern domination of the federal government. When the South seceded, the Republican agenda was quickly realized. Stiff tariffs were levied to protect manufacturers; the Homestead Act was enacted to provide farmers with free land, provided only that they settle on it; and statutes were written committing the government to the construction of a transcontinental railroad. In those same wartime years, the Republicans also put through legislation establishing a national currency and facilitating the importation of skilled foreign labor.

The effect of the last measure was the first to become apparent when the War ended. A million and a half veterans began looking for work after Appomattox, just as war production ceased, only to find themselves competing for scarce jobs with half a million eager immigrants. During the first postwar summer and fall, Union veterans in faded blue uniforms could be seen begging on trolleys and ferryboats, or standing on street corners playing the hurdy-gurdy for pennies.

But the economy was only temporarily depressed as it made the transition from war to peace; soon there were enough jobs for the veterans and the immigrants as well. Recovery occurred most quickly in the farm states. "Notwithstanding the return of so many soldiers, there is a great scarcity of labor in this section," reported the Hudson, Wisconsin *Star* in the fall of 1865. Between 1865 and 1870, Minnesota's population almost doubled in size to 440,000, yet all the while

employment remained high. The Sanitary Commission — which played a charitable role in finding jobs for veterans — noted proudly that only two placement offices had to be opened west of the Alleghenies.

To find their livelihood, many ex-soldiers pushed even farther afield. They ventured into the far western territories being opened by the railroads or into the Southern states, where they had served during the War. Northern initiative, they were convinced, could transform the sluggish Southern economy. "This is an ancient, historic and stupid place," wrote Captain George Whitfield Pepper, an Ohioan visiting Petersburg, Virginia. "Northern pluck and enterprise will make it a prosperous commercial city." Horace Greeley, the champion of westward expansion, even amended his famous dictum advising young men to go west. In an editorial in his New York *Tribune* titled "Southward Ho!", Greeley proclaimed that the choicest lands were actually in the South.

The feverishly accelerating industrial economy of the North created the greatest number of jobs. In the first five years after Appomattox, 360,000 new jobs were created in six major industries. By 1869, there were nearly twice as many manufacturing establishments in the country as had existed only 10 years earlier. The economic momentum gained in the War — with its insatiable demand for such basics as iron, munitions, food, clothing, shoes and transportation — was hardly affected by the surrender at Appomattox. After surveying postwar economics, the astonished Senator Sherman wrote to his brother the general that "they talk of millions as confidently as formerly of thousands."

The enormous profits of the war years,

Genuine Connellsville Coke

VIEW OF DRAVO WORKS.

VIEW OF TROTTER SHAFT.

MINING COAL.

Watering and Drawing Coke.

5000 OVENS, CAPACITY 8750 TONS DAILY.

Process of Manufacturing Coke at the Works of the
H.C. FRICK COKE COMPANY,
CONNELLSVILLE COKE REGION PENNA
POST OFFICE, PITTSBURGH PA.

A lithograph of a Pennsylvania coke works illustrates the heating process used to turn coal into coke, a vital ingredient in steelmaking. Henry Clay Frick, who owned this plant as well as large tracts of Pennsylvania's coal-rich land, sold his holdings in 1882 to steel magnate Andrew Carnegie, who thus ensured a steady supply of coke for his steel mills.

along with the complex financial and production strategies developed to maintain the Union armies, inspired new, large-scale methods for monopolizing peacetime markets. In industry after industry, small family establishments began to disappear, absorbed by great corporations with access to immense capital. For their plants, these corporations sought places where inexpensive lake, river and rail transport made it easy for them to bring together raw materials and sources of energy. The day of the isolated factory run by water power was ending; the age of smoky manufacturing cities such as Fall River, Bridgeport, Paterson, Scranton, Youngstown and Akron had begun.

The sheer quantity of American consumer goods astonished foreign visitors. Using new techniques of mass production, one workman could turn out 300 pairs of shoes in a day, and a single Massachusetts factory could boast that its production equaled that of 30,000 bootmakers. The clothing industry, which had learned during the War to mass-produce uniforms, now filled the stores with inexpensive, standard-size suits. The number of agricultural equipment factories shrank by half, but the productivity of the remaining plants increased by more than 3,000 percent.

Indispensable to this soaring productivity was the adoption of literally hundreds of labor-saving inventions. The surge in clothing production was dependent on the invention of a mechanical cloth cutter, and the boom in shoe production was made possible by New

# The Golden Age of Invention

The coming of peace triggered a burst of inventiveness without parallel in American history. Between 1865 and the turn of the century, the government issued an astounding number of patents — nearly 600,000 of them. Licensed were gadgets, tools and machines related to all areas of human endeavor, from communications and manufacturing to the domestic arts. Every man-made object, it seemed, was examined afresh to see if it could be improved upon; every task was scrutinized to find a faster, safer, cheaper or more efficient method.

Individually, the contributions of most of these devices were hardly monumental. But many of the inventions were tied to the great industries of the day; collectively, they played a dominant role in changing society and the nation's economy by facilitating mass production, increased productivity and swift industrial expansion. Several examples of these minor marvels are shown here.

Thomas Edison's 1873 printing telegraph sent messages six times faster than its predecessor and did not require a Morse code operator. Messages, transmitted by pressing the typewriter-like keys of the telegraph, were printed out in letters on a paper tape at the receiving end.

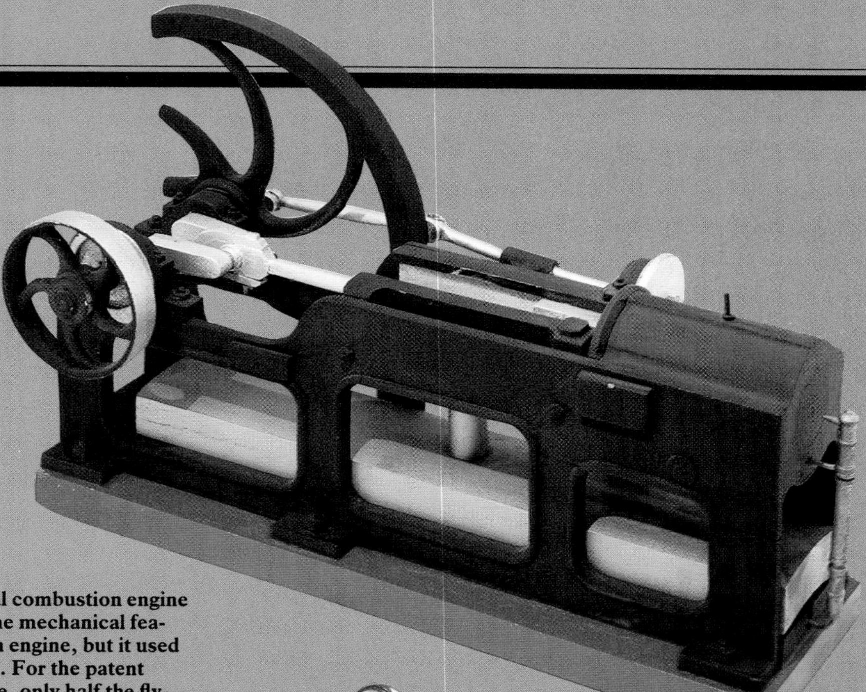

This 1873 internal combustion engine incorporated some mechanical features of the steam engine, but it used petroleum as fuel. For the patent model shown here, only half the flywheel was built to keep it within limits set by the U.S. Patent Office.

Shoemaking was among the first American crafts to become mechanized, and the 1860 sole-cutting machine below helped meet the growing demand for mass-produced footwear during and after the Civil War. Customers paid less for machine-made shoes, and many of them pronounced the shoes more attractive and comfortable than those made by hand.

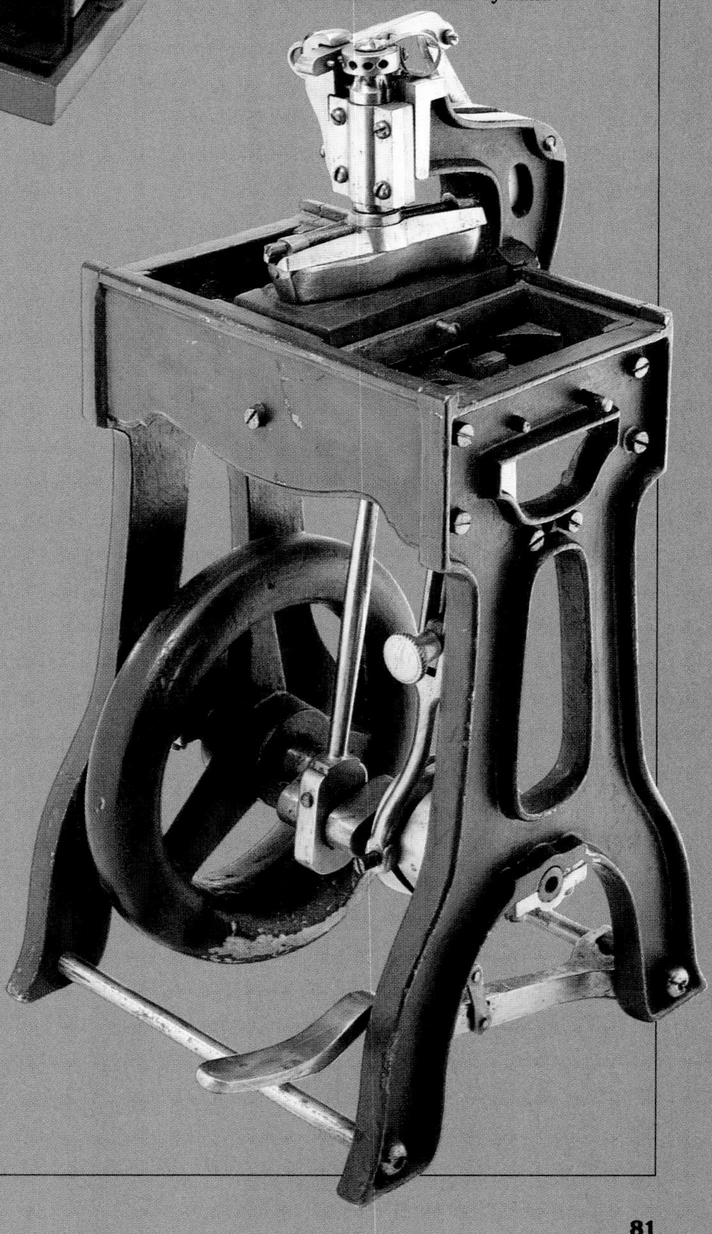

Precision metalworking machines were central to American manufacturing, and John A. Peer's 1874 gear-cutting device (*above*) had many industrial applications. The machine, shown here as a patent model, cut gears of varying sizes and shapes for use in the workings of locomotives, textile machinery and farming equipment.

Englander Gordon McKay's invention of an improved sole-sewing machine. The efficiency of business offices was greatly enhanced by the advent of the first commercial typewriter patented in 1868 by Milwaukeean Christopher Sholes. Domestic routine was transformed by the introduction of washing machines and by the new popularity of sewing machines, which by the end of 1866 sold at the rate of a thousand a day.

In 1872, a 38-year-old ironmaster named Andrew Carnegie made a fateful trip to Great Britain. There he saw the English inventor Henry Bessemer — whom he took to be a "crazy Frenchman" — force air through molten iron, producing a shower of sparks and a flow of white-hot steel. Carnegie rushed home proclaiming that the day of iron was past and that the blast furnace was king. "Give it thirty thousand pounds of common pig iron," he marveled, "and presto! the whole mass is blown into steel."

In fact, the Bessemer process predated the Civil War by a few years, and small quantities of steel had been rolled in the United States since the War's end. Several entrepre-

neurs already were in the business when Carnegie became interested. Surrounding himself with skillful lieutenants, he made up for his late start by negotiating for cheap rail transport and by then constructing the biggest complex of steel properties — including steelmaking plants, rolling mills and bridgeworks — ever assembled under one management. So ardent was Carnegie for savings that he once tore down a barely completed steel mill and rebuilt it, because he had learned of a different design that would save 50 cents per ton.

Establishing his headquarters in Pittsburgh, with ready access to iron ore, soft coal and coke, Carnegie began producing steel in such quantity, and at such low cost, that he drove most of his competitors out of business. Yet in the decade after 1867, American steel production rose from 2,600 tons to 500,000 tons per year.

The growth of the oil industry was even more dramatic. Oil production had begun in 1859 with the drilling of the first well near Titusville, in northwestern Pennsylvania. By the War's end, hundreds of derricks had sprouted in the Titusville area, and the oil boom was on. The man who saw most shrewdly how to take advantage of this development was a pious and secretive young dealer in grain and produce named John Davison Rockefeller, who had decided early that it was better "to let money be my slave than to be the slave of money."

In 1863, Rockefeller took the considerable profits he had amassed by selling provisions to the Army and began investing the money in oil. He regarded drilling as risky, but he saw another avenue to wealth. Almost alone among business leaders, he realized that control of the so-called industrial "narrows" —

the slaughterhouses, milling plants and factories where raw materials were transformed into consumer goods — meant virtual control of an industry.

Rockefeller set out to control the narrows of the oil industry — the refineries. He negotiated from the railroads secret freight rebates that gave his Standard Oil Company of Ohio an overwhelming competitive edge over companies paying regular rates. Within months all 25 of his Cleveland oil-refining competitors were forced to sell out to him at bargain prices.

Shareholders in the failed companies handed over their securities and power to the first of the great industrial "trusts" — powerful monopolies that controlled production and set prices in their territories. By the end of the 1870s, Standard Oil was delivering only two percent of the 26 million barrels of crude oil produced in the country each year; but it was refining 95 percent and dictating the price of all of it. Leaders in other industries — Charles A. Pillsbury in flour milling, Philip D. Armour and Gustavus F. Swift in meat packing, Jay Cooke in finance — were quick to follow Rockefeller's lead. They set up their own alliances to establish production and pricing policies that removed the risk of failure from their enterprises.

The success of these combinations, and that of the booming American economy in general, depended on the railroads. "From the moment that railways were introduced," remarked Henry Adams, "life took on extravagance." Iron rails and steam locomotives opened the West and created the great national market that made mass production not only possible but essential. In the decade after the War, railroad mileage more than doubled, while shipping charges dropped.

Presidential nominee, Ulysses S. Grant (*left of center*), and senior Army generals, including Philip H. Sheridan (*third from left*) and William T. Sherman (*center*), meet with Union Pacific officials at Fort Sanders, Wyoming, in 1868 to settle a routing dispute during the building of the transcontinental railroad. The Union Pacific's chief engineer, former General Grenville M. Dodge (*far left*), had proposed an economical direct route; other officials advocated a complex line requiring larger government loans. Grant made the final decision, and Dodge's view prevailed.

Acutely conscious of the economic impact of the railroads, the state and federal governments gave them unprecedented support. In all, the railroads received 183 million acres of public land, comprising an area more than four times the size of New England. Beyond that, the railroads received government loans totaling $150 million and tax exemptions worth millions more. The most favored beneficiaries were the Union Pacific and the Central Pacific railroads, whose race across the continent toward each other occupied the place in newspaper headlines once reserved for major battles of the War.

The Union Pacific and Central Pacific began laying track in earnest in 1867, jumping off from Omaha and Sacramento respectively. In their haste to outstrip each other, they completed as many as five miles a day when working in favorable terrain. But where the Central Pacific route crossed the Sierras at an altitude of more than 7,000 feet, the Chinese

A champagne toast and a handshake between chief engineers Samuel Montague of the Central Pacific (center, left) and Grenville Dodge of the Union Pacific mark a stirring moment in the opening of the American West — completion of the first transcontinental railroad on May 10, 1869. A symbolic spike of gold was driven into place where the converging rails met, at Promontory in northern Utah.

the army to the railroads — were organized into paramilitary units under the direction of the Union Pacific's chief engineer, Grenville M. Dodge, a former Union general. While they worked, the rail crews "stacked their arms," Dodge explained, "and were ready at a moment's warning to fall in and fight."

At night the men returned to portable towns that every few weeks were dismantled, packed on freight cars and moved — houses, stores, saloons, dance halls and all — to keep pace with the thrust of the railway. Samuel Bowles of the Springfield, Massachusetts *Republican*, visited one rowdy terminal town in 1868 and christened it "Hell on wheels."

On May 10, 1869, engines of the two rival railroads touched cowcatchers at Promontory, Utah — "facing on a single track," in Western writer Bret Harte's words, with "half a world behind each back." The event was toasted with champagne and celebrated with ringing church bells and blaring bands in cities across the land. Completion of the first transcontinental railroad, said the New York *Tribune*, was no less important than the Declaration of Independence, the emancipation of the slaves or the acquisition of California. And General Dodge exclaimed, in tribute to the railroad's seemingly limitless reach, "This is the way to India."

Hyperbole aside, the juncture at Promontory reduced the time required to travel coast to coast from 30 days to seven or eight. Even more important, it triggered the construction of an enormous network of connecting railroads that opened the plains and mountains to ranchers, farmers and miners.

As if by magic, railroad towns sprang up on the central plains to serve as trading and shipping centers. One awed observer described the process: "You may stand ankle

coolies employed by the railroad had to build trestles, culverts, snowsheds, tanks and drainage systems. In one 60-mile stretch, they blasted out no fewer than 15 tunnels. Progress under such conditions slowed to a mere 20 miles a year.

The 12,000 mostly Irish laborers working for the Union Pacific faced less daunting construction problems but a far greater risk of attack by Indians. The workers — many of them veterans who had gone directly from

deep in the short grass of the uninhabited wilderness; next month a train will glide over the waste and stop at some point where the railroad has decided to locate a town. Men, women and children will jump out, and their chattels will tumble out after them. From that moment the building begins."

The effect of the railroads on the nation's economy was incalculable. When more locomotives started burning coal instead of wood, the country's coal production tripled; when the railroads decided to use rails made of steel, the modern steel industry was born. It was the development by the railroads of the refrigerated freight car, in collaboration with Gustavus Swift, that created the meat-packing industry.

The great autocrats of railroading — men such as Collis P. Huntington and Leland Stanford, who in partnership built the Central Pacific and controlled the Southern Pacific — could make an industry or ruin a community merely by changing freight rates. They had more money at their disposal than did many state governments, and they regularly evaded taxation and regulation by coercing and bribing state legislatures. Railroad managers had such power that businessmen routinely sought their approval before launching any enterprise that depended on transportation.

As the financial stakes in railroading became steadily higher, competition became ruinous. The aging shipping magnate Cornelius Vanderbilt, who liked to boast that he had made a million dollars for every year of his life, saw a new kind of opportunity in railroading. He noted that travel by rail from New York to Chicago required frequent changes and the use of as many as a dozen lines, each of them in fierce competition with the others. He began buying railroads until he had forged a single system running from New York to Chicago and on to Omaha — in all, 4,500 miles of track.

Other entrepreneurs followed Vanderbilt's lead, buying and consolidating until there were but four principal railroad routes between the East Coast and the Middle West. Not content with their preeminence, the owners of the large trunk lines went on to forge a series of predatory, monopolistic agreements designed to increase profits and eliminate competition.

In an antimonopoly pamphlet published at the height of railroad consolidation, the embattled farmers of Kansas pinned the label "robber barons" on the aggressive men who ran the railroads. Soon the term was applied to all of the great entrepreneurs of the postwar period — the creators of a new style of unbridled capitalism.

Most of these tycoons had been born in the 1830s and 1840s and had been old enough to fight in the Civil War; few of them, however, had done so. Some would attempt to explain their absence from the battlefield — Rockefeller always insisted that by paying for not one but three substitutes he had tripled his service to the Union — but most took the attitude of financier Thomas Mellon that "only greenhorns enlist."

As a group, the new captains of industry were shrewd, hard-working men, imbued with a faith in progress that was shared by many less successful Americans. Anybody could get ahead, insisted Rockefeller, if the person had "the knack of economy, thrift and perseverance." Carnegie agreed, and he added a comforting thought adapted from the new evolutionary doctrines of Charles Darwin: Those who became rich were obvi-

This elegantly appointed parlor car was typical of first-class accommodations on the nation's railways in the 1870s. Those unable to afford such luxury had to settle for cramped, uncomfortable seats in second class or wooden benches in third class; a reporter for *Frank Leslie's Illustrated Newspaper* described those travelers as "a congregation of aching spines."

ously the best fitted for wealth, because competition "insures the survival of the fittest in every department." Like his fellow entrepreneurs, Carnegie never stopped professing his faith in competition: "It is best for the race," he said, although the trusts through which he conducted most of his business did everything in their power to suppress it.

The robber barons — men such as Jay Gould, Jim Fisk, J. P. Morgan, James J. Hill — made fortunes that were enormous by any standards. Gould had an income of $10 million a year and Carnegie an income of $25 million. Rockefeller at the height of his career was worth more than $815 million. The princely educational and religious charities of the robber barons reflected both a desire to buy respectability and a conviction shared with Rockefeller that "the power to make money is a gift of God" that thus entailed responsibilities.

In their daily lives, the barons gave America a spectacle of conspicuous consumption unlike any the country had ever seen. They traveled in private railroad trains and imported the interiors of European castles to adorn their mansions. Their art collections were the beginnings of the nation's great public museums. At their lavish, fancy-dress balls, the barons outdid one another with such gestures as folding in each dinner napkin a bracelet made of solid gold for the ladies, or enclosing a black pearl in each serving of oysters, or passing around cigars wrapped in $100 bills.

Henry Adams thought the lives of the colossally rich were "no more worth living than those of their cooks," but the barons' exploits amazed and inspired the ambitious young men of the new middle class. Andrew Carnegie's essay on how to succeed,

"The Gospel of Wealth," was their guide. In 1867, a former Unitarian minister named Horatio Alger made his literary debut with a book called *Ragged Dick*. In this best seller, and in the hundred that followed, Alger espoused initiative and hard work, and preached that material success was a sign of virtue. It was a highly palatable message at a time when Americans were enjoying better food, clothing, housing and education than before the War, as well as comforts once reserved only for the rich.

Yet large numbers of Americans benefited little from the process of industrialization, and many even suffered because of it. Prominent among these groups were the workers in the nation's increasingly mechanized factories. Although wages rose by 60 percent between 1860 and 1866, Revenue Commissioner David A. Wells observed that the cost of living increased by close to 100 percent in the same period.

Conditions in many factories and mercantile establishments were appalling. A 10-hour day was normal, and a 12-to-18-hour day was not uncommon. Young women in urban dry goods stores often worked from seven-thirty in the morning until ten at night, with no place to sit down and no toilets available to them. A man might earn two dollars a day, but women rarely received more than $3.50 a week. Moreover, testified a textile worker in Fall River, Massachusetts, "There is no redress here, and no appeal. The by-word is 'If you don't like it, get out!' " Another factory hand compared the warlike animosity between worker and employer to "the former feeling of bitterness between the North and South."

Unable to afford decent housing, workers crowded into urban shantytowns and tene-

Shantytowns such as this one in Central Park provided the only housing available to many of New York City's poor and to the immigrants who arrived in record numbers after the War. When the sprawling slums began to encroach on New York's wealthier neighborhoods, one visitor compared the city to "a lady at a costume ball, with diamonds in her ears and her toes out at her boots."

ment buildings in which four people or more occupied a single, often windowless room. Sanitation was so rudimentary that thousands died of typhoid, smallpox and scarlet fever. In Boston, more than a fifth of the population — 60,000 people — were jammed into 2,800 registered tenements. New York was so ill-prepared for the postwar flood of immigration that a fifth of its 100,000 slum dwellers were forced to live in cellars.

The workers tried to improve their lot by organizing trade unions. During the 1860s, these were nonmilitant organizations largely concerned with setting up cooperative factories owned by the workers. But they soon became far more combative.

By the 1870s, more than 30 national unions had come into being, with a total membership of roughly 300,000. They agitated for such goals as an eight-hour workday, compulsory arbitration, equal pay for men and women, and a ban on child and convict labor. Although most of the unions were conservative by European standards, they were regarded suspiciously by much of

the general public as unpatriotic and dangerously radical. Their greatest sin, in the view of one probusiness publication, was that they crippled "the productive power of capital."

The conflict between workers and managers inevitably led to violence. One notable outbreak involved the Molly Maguires — a secretive society of Irish-American miners who were accused of waging a war of assassination and property destruction against owners and foremen in the anthracite coal fields of eastern Pennsylvania. In the mid-1870s, management agitated for a repressive campaign of strict law enforcement against all labor unions, and 20 Molly Maguires were hanged for murder. Violence of this kind, together with management's resort to immigrant labor and the squeeze of hard times, led to a decline in the labor movement. By the end of the decade only eight or nine national unions were left, and they were almost without funds.

The traditional problems of the nation's farmers were also compounded by the new age. The massive migration to the plains, as

well as the introduction of labor saving farm machinery — steam-traction engines, mechanical reapers and binders — led inevitably to overproduction and a glut on the world market. While prices plummeted, the railroads raised their rates to exorbitant levels. To ship a bushel of corn from Nebraska to Chicago in 1877 cost one half the sale price of the corn. The railroad companies also owned many of the grain elevators and routinely cheated farmers by classifying grain below its actual grade.

Angry farmers soon formed cooperative buying and selling associations, many of which were clustered under an umbrella organization known as the Patrons of Husbandry, or Grange. By lobbying for "Granger laws," farmers managed to get fixed freight rates and warehouse charges in a half-dozen states. But the laws were easily evaded, and the producers of staple crops continued to be one of the depressed groups of the postwar era.

Nevertheless, the lure of the plains and the dream of agrarian independence continued to pull Americans westward throughout the Reconstruction period. The population of the west-central states — Minnesota, Iowa, Nebraska, Kansas, Missouri and the Dakota territory — almost tripled between 1860 and 1880. An Eastern journalist traveling on horseback across the Great Plains in 1866 found to his astonishment that the trails seemed as crowded as the highways back East. In 1865 General Dodge, then in command of the Department of the Missouri, estimated that wagons were crossing the plains at a rate of 5,000 per month.

The principal spur to this westward migration was the Homestead Act of 1862, un-

Members of a Nebraska family, and their livestock, gather outside their sod house, which was typical of the shelters built by homesteaders in the treeless plains. Life in an earthen house had its drawbacks — a leaky roof was the most disagreeable feature — but the structure itself was durable enough to last seven or eight years, and it was well-insulated against the extremes of heat and cold that afflicted the region.

der which a person could become the owner of 160 acres in return for five years of occupancy and improvements. Ownership was made even easier for veterans: An 1864 supplement to the Homestead Act offered them choice land and reduced the residence requirement to one year. Settlers who did not claim land under the Homestead Act could buy it from the states or from railway companies for five to ten dollars an acre. In each of the years immediately after the War, five to seven million acres of public lands were thus sold or granted.

The vast majority of men and women who settled the Great Plains were people of modest means — war veterans; clerks and artisans; immigrants from Germany, Scandinavia and elsewhere in Europe. Their new life was, at least at first, a nightmarish ordeal. The pioneers were vulnerable to sporadic Indian attacks, tornadoes, grass fires and brutal winter weather.

Homesteaders on the wind-swept prairie found few trees to provide them with lumber; they had to construct their houses with blocks of sod sourly referred to as "Nebraska marble." For fuel, farmers had to depend on dried buffalo dung, corn cobs or dried grass. Water was perennially scarce, except during deluges of rain that washed away earth and crops. Winter blizzards and summer dust storms whipped the lonely farms. Locusts periodically swarmed over the fields, stripping the wheat and corn and sometimes obscuring the sun. Always there was the danger of prairie fires that raced like the wind through the tall grass. Most men went armed to protect their families and their livestock from marauding Indians, and from wolves and other predators.

Many gave up. "I came to the conclusion," said a homesteader who quit, "that any man who would leave the luxuries of a boardinghouse, where they had hash every day, to lay Nebraska sod was a fool." By the end of the 1870s, nearly a half million families had moved West to stake their claims, but fewer than half of them had completed the five-year residence requirement and had taken permanent possession.

The immigrant homesteaders also had to contend with the cattlemen, whose range country they crisscrossed with their fences and irrigation ditches. Many of the pioneer cattlemen were army veterans who came home to the Nueces valley region of southwest Texas to find wild cattle flourishing on the grassy plain. Left unattended when the Texans went off to fight for the Confederacy, the cattle had multiplied so prodigiously that there were said to be nearly five million of them by the end of the Civil War.

With the thrust of the railways across the northern ranges, a whole new market opened to Texas cattlemen. In vast herds of as many as 10,000 head, the longhorns were driven from the sparse Texas range into Kansas, Missouri, Arkansas, Nebraska and Colorado, there to fatten on fertile northern pasture lands before being shipped by rail to the packing houses of the Midwest. At the railheads, cow towns such as Abilene, Newton and Dodge City soon mushroomed into rowdy, violent marketplaces.

The cattle drive in its heyday — from 1865 to about 1879 — yielded enormous profits. During that time, nearly four million longhorns moved up the cattle trails. A smart operator could buy them in Texas for three or four dollars a head and sell them for 10 times that amount in northern markets.

But the days of the Long Drive were soon

over. The homesteaders fiercely opposed the drives, which trampled their crops and infected their livestock with Texas fever, carried by the longhorns. The invention of barbed wire in 1874 gave the settlers a means of protecting their croplands and water holes, and federal legislation gradually closed off vast portions of the range. By the end of the 1870s, practically all of Kansas and Nebraska were off-limits to the trail herds. Thereafter the cattlemen created permanent ranches in Texas and on the Great Plains, where herds could graze on public lands within easy reach of the expanding railway system.

While ranching and farming drew people to the plains, mining beckoned them to the far western states. The search for mineral riches had begun with the California gold rush in 1849 and had reached a climax during and just after the War. By railroad, riverboat, covered wagon and mule, prospectors invaded the western mountain country in search of gold and silver. In the wild, inhospitable regions between California and the Dakota Territory, the prospectors gathered in agglomerations of wagons, lean-tos, tents and kennels burrowed into the hillsides. Among the permanent cities born in this manner were Denver, Colorado; Butte, Montana; and Boise, Idaho.

Life in such towns was rough and dangerous. An English traveler, W. Hepworth Dixon, concluded when he visited Denver that he had arrived in "a city of demons." Men were shot outside his window, and every night there were brawls in the saloons and gambling dens. Desperadoes popularly known as "road agents" roamed the rough arteries between towns, intercepting coaches that might be bearing gold dust and some-

times killing the driver and passengers. Denver was only one of many communities where citizens took the law into their own hands and began hanging bandits from telegraph poles and cottonwood trees.

All told, the mining strikes of the prewar and postwar years enriched the country by more than two billion dollars and vastly accelerated the settlement of the mountainous West. The last major strike in the United States of the time occurred in the Black Hills of the Dakota Territory, in 1874. Miners began pouring into the Dakota hills after Lieutenant Colonel George Armstrong Custer reconnoitered the area with a thousand troopers of the 7th Cavalry, ostensibly to find a site for a fort. In his initial report, Custer said he had found "gold among the roots of the grass." Though Custer later toned down his claim, so many miners came rushing up the Missouri River to follow the trail Custer's supply wagons had cut that the resident Sioux began calling the route "Thieves' Road."

Custer and the miners were intruding on territory given to the Sioux in perpetuity by the U.S. government in 1868. The Black Hills incursion was one more chapter in the troubled history of relations between Indians and whites. "We have come to this point in the history of the country," said Maine Senator Lot M. Morrill two years after the Civil War ended. "There is no place beyond population to which you can remove the Indian."

Morrill's statement starkly summarized the dilemma of an expansionist society confronted by a people whose culture was bound to the earth. One administration after another had evaded the problem by forcing the Indians ever farther west. Now space was running out, and the question had to be

Nat Love, a former Tennessee slave, was one of many blacks who exchanged the uncertainties of life in the postwar South for the relative freedom and new opportunities available in the West. As a $30-a-month cowpuncher, Love learned on the job how to ride, rope and shoot — skills most black cowboys had acquired as slaves on Texas ranches.

Rome: "One of our hands holds the rifle and the other the peace-pipe, and we blaze away with both instruments at the same time."

In the decade following Appomattox, the shrunken U.S. Army fought more than 200 engagements with Indians in a campaign to secure the frontier. At the time there were 225,000 Indians west of the Mississippi, comprising more than 30 distinct tribes. Of these, the most powerful and the most restless were the Sioux, the Arapahoe, the Cheyenne and the Comanche. These so-called "horse Indians" fought a kind of continuous mounted warfare that at its peak engaged 25,000 U.S. troops.

In 1864, a massacre of peace-seeking Cheyenne at Sand Creek by Colorado militia sparked a general uprising. The vengeful Cheyenne and Sioux went on the warpath across much of Wyoming and Montana in 1865, and by the following year they were strong enough to wipe out a cavalry detachment from Fort Phil Kearny and to endanger other military posts. In 1868, the Cheyenne, Comanche, Kiowa and other tribes of the southern plains intensified their attacks on travel routes along the Texas frontier between the Red River and El Paso. In response, the 7th Cavalry serving under Custer surrounded a Cheyenne village along the Washita River in November 1868 and slaughtered 103 warriors and 40 women and children. Among the dead was Chief Black Kettle, a leading proponent of peace and a survivor of the Sand Creek massacre.

The ascending spiral of violence, with barbarities perpetrated on both sides, fueled demands for a more constructive Indian policy. An eight-member Peace Commission that was appointed in 1867 studied the situation and concluded that Indians and whites

faced head on: The government must either establish an "abiding place" for the Indian tribes, observed Senator Morrill, or exterminate them and appropriate the last of their hunting grounds.

Instead, as the struggle for the West unfolded, the U.S. government equivocated. It approached the Indians "Janus-faced," wrote an editor of the *Army and Navy Journal,* referring to the two-faced god of ancient

# Photographer
# of the Virgin West

The little that most Americans of the 1860s knew about the mysterious region "out West" came from the wildly embellished tales of returning adventurers. Seeking more reliable information, the government sent teams of explorers to survey the western territories and record their observations. Many of the classic photographs that resulted from these expeditions were the work of a young Irish-American named Timothy O'Sullivan.

O'Sullivan had begun his career as an apprentice to Mathew Brady, who in 1861 outfitted him with a portable darkroom and dispatched him to cover the War. The apprentice grew into an intrepid field photographer with an artist's eye for detail. In 1867, he was invited to join the survey team of geologist Clarence King, and in 1871 he went on an expedition led by Lieutenant George Wheeler. In all, O'Sullivan spent seven years traversing the frontier, where he produced more than 1,000 images of a West more spectacular than anything the tale-spinners had imagined.

As shy in front of the camera as he was comfortable behind it, O'Sullivan rarely posed for photographs. This *carte de visite* was probably made in late 1868, when he returned to Washington, D.C., for a few months to print the results of his first expedition to the West.

Captivated by the "wildness of beauty" at Idaho's Shoshone Falls in 1868, O'Sullivan photographed a member of the King expedition standing on a cliff overlooking the 212-foot cascade (*above*).

O'Sullivan's 1873 photograph of the imposing walls of the Canyon de Chelly in Arizona shows pueblo ruins that were built centuries before into a large cavity 60 feet above the canyon's bed. Each stratum of the rock wall, which towers almost 1,000 feet above the valley, is boldly outlined by brilliant sunlight.

Taken from atop a dune, this 1867 photograph embraces the undulating sands of the California desert, broken only by O'Sullivan's footprints leading from the mule-drawn wagon that was his darkroom. "A feeling pervades the mind," he wrote, "that you are, if not the first white man who has ever trod that trail, certainly one of the few who have ventured so far."

could not live in close proximity without warfare. The result was a series of treaties that moved the Indians away from the railways and settled them on reservations, the largest of which comprised significant portions of present-day Arizona, New Mexico and South Dakota.

Surprisingly, the treaties secured two years of comparative peace. But then the Indians began wandering back to their old hunting grounds, and whites began invading protected Indian lands that contained previously unsuspected mineral wealth. In 1871, Congress voted to no longer recognize Indian tribes as "domestic dependent nations" and henceforth to make all Indians answerable to U.S. laws.

Far from heeding such laws, most of the tribes continued to resort to violence — the Kiowa, Cheyenne and Comanche in the Red River War of 1874-1875, and the Sioux

and northern Cheyenne in "Sitting Bull's war" of 1876-1877.

Eventually the Sioux and northern Cheyenne would be forced back to their reservations — but only after the annihilation of Custer and five companies of his regiment at the Little Big Horn on June 25, 1876. By the end of that year, the Indian uprisings would be contained, except for sporadic outbursts that would continue for another 15 years.

Meanwhile, however, the nation's Indian policy stirred heated dispute. To Westerners who lived under threat of Indian attack and had firsthand experience with Indian atrocities, the only possible policy seemed one of military force. "I only wish," wrote an army wife in 1874, "those people who are so opposed to fighting the Indian could come out here & live, or have some relative scalped. Then they would soon find the true & only way to do with them is to kill, kill." To East-

A delegation of peacemakers meets with tribal chiefs in 1868 at Fort Laramie, Wyoming. Although General Sherman *(third from left, under the tent)* helped negotiate the resulting treaties, he grumbled that in order to ensure peace the Indians would "all have to be killed or maintained as a species of paupers."

ern churchmen and reformers, including many former abolitionists, such attitudes were appalling. The reformers' ideal was to "civilize" Indians and receive them into the body politic of the nation. Either policy ensured that the Indians could not live as they had lived before.

Among those who understood the dilemma most cogently was Francis A. Walker, a former Union officer whom Grant had appointed Commissioner of Indian Affairs. "Every year's advance of our frontier," he wrote, "takes in a territory as large as some of the kingdoms of Europe. We are richer by hundreds of millions, the Indian is poorer by a large part of the little that he has. This growth is bringing imperial greatness to the nation; to the Indian it brings wretchedness, destitution, beggary." Yet Walker, like many other well-meaning Northerners, saw no way to halt a process that was so intimately linked to the nation's expansion. As long as gold was to be found in Indian territory, Senator John Sherman reminded his colleagues, the "wave of emigration" would roll on into tribal lands even if "the whole army of the United States stood in the way."

Meantime, most of the nation had little attention to spare for Indian affairs. For many Americans, the economic activity and financial opportunities of the postwar era obscured and made irrelevant the deadly turmoil not only in the Indian territories, but in the states of the former Confederacy.

"The Northern mind being active, and full of what is called progress, runs away from the past," wrote the crusading Attorney General of the Grant Administration, Amos Akerman. "Even such atrocities as Ku-Kluxery do not hold their attention." The atrocities to which Akerman referred were the response of the white South to the imposition in the late 1860s of Radical Reconstruction, with its provisions for black voting rights and resultant Republican governments. Those who ignored what was happening included, for a time, the newly elected President Grant.

Even as the recalcitrant states were being impressed back into the Union, the forces of counter-Reconstruction were erupting. During the election campaign of 1868, more than a thousand persons, most of them black, were killed in Louisiana alone. The following year, 163 blacks were murdered in a single Florida county. The primary agencies behind this unbridled mayhem were the Ku Klux Klan and such similar groups as the New Orleans-based Knights of the White Camelia. Night riders clad in sheets also burned scores of black schools, determined to stamp out what the Klan called "free-nigger education." Carpetbaggers and scalawags found threatening notes, adorned with drawings of skulls or coffins, nailed to their front doors. "Beware," read a typical warning, "thy end is nigh. Dead, dead, under the roses."

While the federal government and the Northern states got on with the business of progress, the Southern state governments tried desperately to save themselves. Beginning with Tennessee in 1868, they proscribed the Klan with a series of so-called "Ku Klux Laws." The laws banned membership in secret societies that disturbed the peace and made the sheltering of night riders a crime. Some even outlawed the wearing of a mask in public: Under an Alabama statute, the fact that a man hid his face and wore a costume became *prima facie* evidence of guilt. But the state governments lacked the power and the civilian support that was necessary to enforce the new laws effectively, and the Klan raged on.

Beginning in March of 1869, Congress reacted to the worsening situation by repealing the prohibition on state militias in the Southern states. However, the troops raised by the governors and sent against the Klan not only failed to control the situation but often made it worse; many of the militiamen organized by the Radical Republican governments were black, and their use of force against whites further inflamed the hatreds.

In March of 1870, the last of the required three fourths of the states ratified the 15th Amendment to the Constitution, guaranteeing the vote to blacks in every state. The Amendment had been bulldozed through by the Republicans to make sure that Southern blacks would retain the vote should Democrats return to power there, and to end the untenable situation in which blacks were guaranteed the right to vote in former Confederate states but denied it in 16 Northern states. With the Amendment ratified, many people declared the problems of Reconstruction solved. It was, said the American Anti-Slavery Society, the "completion of our movement, the fulfillment of our pledge to the Negro race."

But by that time, Republican leaders in Congress already knew that much more would be required. Without additional federal laws to bolster the Reconstruction governments, said Senator John Pool of North Carolina, the "whole fabric of Reconstruction, with all the principles connected with it, amounts to nothing at all, and in the end it will topple and fall."

That spring the Congress made interference with voters a federal crime and put such cases under the jurisdiction of federal courts. But the laws and the courts proved impotent, given witnesses who were afraid to testify and jurors afraid to convict. The terror spread, and when it came time for state elections, blacks and those who sympathized with them were too frightened to vote, much less offer themselves as candidates.

Reconstruction Republicans began to disappear from office, replaced by white-supremacist, counter-Reconstruction Democrats. In the fall of 1870, Governor William W. Holden of North Carolina, realizing that he was about to be voted from office thanks to the guns and whips of the Ku Klux Klan, appealed to President Grant for help. There was no reply. Governor Holden was returned to private life.

By the end of the year, however, Grant had become concerned enough to suggest that Congress take further action. A committee investigated and found, in North Carolina as elsewhere, "a carnival of murders, intimidation, and violence of all kinds." By the spring of 1871, South Carolina was in flames to such an extent that Grant became convinced that life, property and government operations in the state were in jeopardy.

Congress tinkered with the ineffective federal laws against civil rights abuse, which did not go far enough to threaten the welfare of the Klan. Then in April it passed an Enforcement Act that went so far it even alarmed some Republicans. The Act declared that the depredations of the Klan constituted rebellion; it gave the President power to oppose the night riders by suspending the writ of habeas corpus and proclaiming martial law wherever he considered it necessary.

Grant was reluctant to use these powers

THE FIFTEENTH AMENDMENT.

CELEBRATED MAY 19TH 1870.

A patriotic lithograph salutes the passage in 1870 of the 15th Amendment to the Constitution, which eliminated "race, color or previous conditon of servitude" as legal barriers to voting. Surrounding the image of blacks holding a celebratory parade are likenesses of early civil rights proponents Frederick Douglass (*top center*), Abraham Lincoln (*lower left*) and John Brown (*lower right*); President Grant and Vice President Schuyler Colfax appear in the upper corners. Other illustrations honor such personal freedoms as religion, education and the sanctity of the family.

because he foresaw the possibility of a new civil war, this one perhaps a racial conflict between blacks and whites. But in October, when Attorney General Akerman declared terrorism in South Carolina to be out of control, Grant was forced to act. He imposed martial law in nine South Carolina counties and sent federal troops into the countryside to round up members of the Klan. Five hundred Klansmen were arrested, of whom 55 were eventually convicted and imprisoned. Similar efforts in Alabama, North Carolina and Mississippi brought similar results, and for a while the violence was quenched.

One of the goals of the Radical Republi-

cans in imposing their brand of Reconstruction had been to create a powerful Republican Party in the South and to prevent the return to power of Southern Democrats. As 1872 approached, and with it a new national election, both the Reconstruction governments and the Republican Party in the South were on the verge of total collapse.

Only vigorous and effective intervention by the federal government, it seemed, could stem the tide of brutality and secure the hard-won rights of the ex-slaves. But even as the government knew it had to save the South, it was ever more paralyzed by a corrosive new enemy — untrammeled corruption.

# Soldiering on the Frontier

For nearly three decades following the Civil War much of the United States Army was engaged in intermittent warfare on the Western Frontier with Indians who fiercely resisted the encroachment of their tribal homelands by the white man. It was hard duty that offered the men little glamor and even less prestige; one Regular disgruntled by the situation wrote that the word "soldier" had become "a synonym for all that is degrading and low."

Most of the men who were stationed on the frontier were prompted by economic rather than patriotic motives. "The large majority," said a veteran officer, "are driven to enlist by absolute want." Promotion was slow, desertion rates in some units ran as high as 30 percent, and the service was plagued with alcoholism, venereal disease and suicide. Yet, for all its faults, the army on the frontier endured the hardships of the Indian wars with a fortitude that earned more than 400 soldiers the Congressional Medal of Honor.

Sergeant Jeremiah Finley (inset), assigned to the U.S. 7th Cavalry in Dakota Territory, and a detachment from the 9th Cavalry (below), a black regiment stationed at Fort Davis, Texas, wear the elaborate full-dress uniforms issued to the cavalry in 1872. Army regulations requiring a daily dress parade were rigidly adhered to, even at isolated posts.

# The Perils of Indian Warfare

On campaign, the frontier soldier was pitted against harsh terrain, inclement weather and a skilled, elusive foe. The physical and psychological demands sometimes proved insurmountable. "I have seen men become so exhausted they were actually insane," one officer recalled; "I saw men who were very plucky sit down and cry like children because they could not hold out." In battle, the soldiers expected no mercy: "Keep the last bullet for yourself" became an unwritten rule of Indian warfare.

Muffled against the cold in buffalo coats, fur headgear and overshoes, Colonel Nelson A. Miles (*center*) and his staff prepare to leave their base on Montana's Tongue River in pursuit of Sioux led by Crazy Horse. On the January day in 1877 that this photograph was taken the temperature stood at 40 degrees below zero.

A centipede-like column of covered wagons, carrying supplies for Lieutenant Colonel George A. Custer's command, rolls through the Black Hills of the Dakota Territory in the summer of 1874. Custer's troops were able to supplement their rations with fish and game obtained from their verdant surroundings.

Hungry soldiers called General George Crook's expedition against the Sioux in the autumn of 1876 the "starvation march." Ailing horses were slaughtered for food for the men, a task four troopers reenacted for a photographer at the expedition's conclusion (*left*).

# A Lonesome Life on the Plains

Home for the western soldier was one of the dozens of small forts that guarded the frontier. Although a busy schedule of drills and fatigue duty kept leisure time to a minimum, loneliness and boredom proved nearly as threatening to the soldier in garrison as Indians were in the field. Drunkenness was rampant and ruined many a promising career. One of the few pleasures of frontier army life was the presence of the soldiers' wives and children, who helped to make the isolation endurable.

Frances Roe, who accompanied her officer husband to the frontier, wears a riding habit modeled on his West Point cadet uniform. A lover of the outdoors, Mrs. Roe called her life in the West "simply glorious."

A soldier at Fort Bridger, Wyoming, is forced to endure humiliation as well as discomfort for a petty infraction in a frontier version of an old army punishment dubbed "riding the wooden horse." Serious breaches of discipline were punished by loss of pay and confinement at hard labor.

Officers of the 7th Cavalry pose proudly with their wives and children at Fort Rice, Dakota Territory, in 1874. One married officer avowed that "to have lived a season together in a frontier post weaves a bond that is never loosened."

A trooper listens to the comforting words of a chaplain moments before being hanged for murder in Prescott, Arizona. Although military justice was harsh on the frontier, the death sentence was invoked less frequently than it had been during the Civil War.

# A Presidency Scarred by Scandal

*"Thoughtful souls are seeking to divine whether it is possible for a democracy to save itself from the corrupting tyranny of capital."*

CONNECTICUT NOVELIST JOHN W. DE FOREST, 1873

The troubled presidency of Ulysses S. Grant bequeathed to the English language two unfortunate terms: Grantism and Black Friday. Each one of these was a shorthand reference to unbridled corruption — in postwar America in general, and in the Grant Administration in particular.

The years of Grant's presidency presented a pathetic spectacle: The aging hero, his integrity and abilities intact, was surrounded and tainted by associates who were incompetent or dishonest, or both. As his longtime subordinate, General George G. Meade, wrote, Grant was an honest man, of "great force of character," pure motives and "unflinching tenacity of purpose." But Meade also observed "a simple and guileless disposition, which is apt to put him, unknown to himself, under the influence of those who should not influence him and desire to do so only for their own purposes."

Most of the men Grant appointed to his original Cabinet and staff were undistinguished (Secretary of State Hamilton Fish being a notable exception); many were corrupt, others were personal friends of Grant's or were members of his family. "Thirteen relations of the President are billeted on the country," fumed Senator Charles Sumner, who added that "this strange abuse did not stop with relatives but widened to include relatives of relatives."

Grant had taken office with his reputation unsullied and had seemed bent on reform — especially of the civil service, with its notorious spoils system, inefficiency and waste. He tried to encourage appointments based on merit rather than on influence or seniority; yet, from the first, his personal loyalty blinded him to incompetence and venality among his close associates. This trait encouraged the national state of affairs that came to be known generically as Grantism.

Another result of what Meade called Grant's "too confident and sanguine disposition" was the infamous Black Friday. The date was Friday, September 24, 1869. For some months, two voracious young financiers — James "Jubilee Jim" Fisk Jr. and Jay Gould — had been advancing a scheme that was anything but a normal reach for reasonable profits; they had been conspiring to exploit the national market in gold.

It was a plot of breathtaking audacity. Fisk and Gould had recently won a vicious financial battle with Cornelius Vanderbilt for control of the Erie Railroad. Enriched by their profits from this contest and emboldened by their success at bribing legislators, suborning a judge and watering stock, the two decided to try their hand at controlling the price of gold, the metal underpinning of the nation's currency.

Their scheme was to buy gold on the New York Stock Exchange until they owned a major portion of the country's supply, refuse to sell any of it until the resulting shortage drove up the price of the metal, then unload their hoard at a fabulous profit. The only problem was that the U.S. Treasury owned a

On the basis of this working model, former slave Charles Thomas Christmas received a patent in 1880 for his invention, a cotton-baling press. Designed to cut shipping costs by making bales more compact, the press was one of hundreds of devices that were patented by blacks in the decades following the War.

great deal of gold — $80 million worth — and could sell enough at any time to hold down the price and wreck the plan.

To neutralize the threat of government intervention, Gould recruited an additional conspirator. He was a 61-year-old lawyer and lobbyist, Abel Rathbone Corbin, who by no coincidence happened to be a brother-in-law of President Grant. At a series of meetings arranged by Corbin during the summer of 1869, Fisk and Gould tried to convince the President that any sudden sale of government gold in the near future — in the event, say, that the price of the metal should begin to climb — would depress farm prices and hurt the Republican Party at the polls.

By September, Gould and Fisk were buying gold in earnest and had spread tales that Mrs. Grant and others close to the President were fellow speculators. The resulting gold fever pushed the price of the metal up to $140 per ounce. Horace Greeley's denunciations of this unsettling activity in New York

*Tribune* editorials aroused Grant's suspicions. Fearing that Grant might yield to public pressure, Corbin — under Gould's guidance — wrote a letter to the President again extolling the benefits of raising the price of gold. In the same letter he confessed his complicity in the affair, hoping that Grant would not ruin a member of his own family. On September 23, Corbin received his answer in a letter to his wife, written by her sister Julia Grant. "Tell your husband that my husband is very much annoyed by your speculations," wrote the First Lady. "You must close them down as quick as you can."

The letter made no mention of selling Treasury gold, but the message was clear. The next morning Gould, warned by Corbin of Grant's intention, quietly sold off his holdings. It is unclear exactly when Fisk learned of the impending catastrophe, but for most of the morning he continued to buy — and the price continued to rise. By 11:53 a.m. it had passed $160. At 11:57 a.m. an order arrived at the Gold Room in New York from the U.S. Treasury, offering for sale four million dollars' worth of gold. As intended, the offer burst the gold-price balloon, which immediately began to fall. Trading erupted in what Fisk later described as "the wildest confusion and the most unearthly screaming of men driven to the verge of temporary insanity by the consciousness of ruin." Fifteen minutes later the price of gold had plummeted by $30 an ounce.

Not "desiring to stay there any longer," Fisk recalled later, he and Gould slipped out by way of a side door. Avoiding a former associate who was now "crazy as a loon," they fled to Fisk's office over the Grand Opera House. The faces of men in the streets of New York's financial district, wrote a newspaper reporter, "made one feel as if Gettysburg had been lost and the rebels were marching down Broadway."

The two miscreants were less worried about their money than about preserving their lives. Gould had sold out that morning at a handsome profit, and Fisk would later simply refuse to honor his contracts to buy gold at the higher prices. A seething mob of ruined speculators converged on the Opera House, threatening death to the brokers of the Gold Ring. Fisk and Gould had to make another clandestine departure, this time by the back stairs.

The specific events of Black Friday soon faded from memory but the term remained, signifying fraud, panic, financial ruin — and collusion in the highest places. No one could forget that, as Speaker of the House James A. Garfield put it, the trail of accountability "led into the parlor of the President."

Other trails in that free-booting age led into other posh parlors: "There is hardly a legislature in the country which is not suspected of corruption," declared *The Nation* in 1868. "There is hardly a court over which the same suspicion does not hang." When lobbyists went to Albany they took along trunks of greenbacks to help New York legislators decide how to vote. In Pennsylvania, people said the Standard Oil Company could do anything it pleased with the legislature except refine it.

It was a time, observed Henry Adams, when men "without character and without credit" could "make levies upon the whole business of the nation." The sheer unabashed magnitude of the corruption astounded Adams and other reformers. The watering of railroad stock was common practice, Navy Yard contracts were padded in

collusion with the Secretary of the Navy, and streetcar franchises went to the bidders who offered the largest bribes to aldermen. Bosses in the big cities distributed coal, flour and cash to the immigrant poor — then told them how to vote. U.S. Senators were openly bankrolled by commercial interests ranging from oil to iron and steel.

Small wonder that the Grant Administration was soon tainted; cartoonists portrayed

Panicky traders in the New York Gold Room try to limit their losses on Black Friday, September 24, 1869, during the currency crisis engineered by Jim Fisk and Jay Gould (*opposite*). The Gold Room's central fountain "serenely spouted and bubbled as usual," wrote one chronicler of the day, while the "money masters" shrieked orders and curses "with savage energy and wildest gesture."

Seemingly mismatched partners, fleshy and jovial James "Jubilee Jim" Fisk Jr. (*above*) and frail, secretive Jay Gould (*right*) teamed up to reap huge profits from deals that ruined countless other investors. The money that the two men made on Black Friday, Fisk later flippantly told a congressional committee, had "gone where the woodbine twineth" — vanished beyond recall.

the President with a bewildered expression, trying to grope his way out of a labyrinth. Certainly he was naive and curiously obtuse in his relations with the business community: For example, he never understood the criticism of his role in the events of Black Friday, and he continued to accept favors from Jim Fisk long afterward.

Some of the numerous scandals that adhered to the Grant Administration — and thus had an indirect but critical impact on the struggling Reconstruction process — were no fault of his. One, the so-called Credit Mobilier Affair, concerned funds voted by Congress for the construction of the Union Pacific Railroad. The exotically named Credit Mobilier was a Pennsylvania construction company formed by Union Pacific stockholders to build the railway. The directors of Credit Mobilier were also directors of the Union Pacific; they set out to milk their own company by grossly overestimating construction costs.

The price of building the railway line quickly rose to $96,000 per mile — three times the estimate made by engineers. All told, $50 million was unaccounted for. Various senators, congressmen and cabinet officers — including Vice President Schuyler Colfax — profited from stock in Credit Mobilier that had been given to them.

Another major scandal that reached a peak during Grant's first term centered on a man remembered simply as Boss Tweed. The depredations of William Marcy Tweed took place far from the office of the presidency but were seen as reflecting the lax moral standards of the Grant Administration. Tweed, in fact, was a Democrat — one of a handful of powerful bosses who ruled the nation's cities as if they were private principalities. If Tweed was the best known of these scoundrels, it was because his thieveries were the most spectacular.

A genial man who weighed nearly 300 pounds, Tweed had a kind of bluff charm that disarmed even his enemies. When he began his larcenous career in the 1860s, one New Yorker in two was an immigrant, and half of the city's residents lived in noxious slums. Violent crime was endemic. Tweed dominated this unruly metropolis for a decade. He bribed police officers, magistrates and the mayor himself; handed out hush money to the city's newspapers; spent $600,000 to sway the members of the state legislature on a single vote for a revised city charter. Tweed's thugs, popularly known as "shoulder-hitters," kept Republican voters away from the polls, and his "repeaters" voted frequently enough to ensure Democratic landslides. In a typical depredation, Tweed charged the city $11 million for a courthouse that cost three million dollars to build, listing thermometers at $7,500 apiece and a plasterer's pay at $133,000 for two day's work. When asked why carpets cost $350,000, one contractor blithely replied, "The carpets in these public buildings need to be changed a great deal oftener than in private houses." All told, Boss Tweed and his accomplices siphoned off an estimated $200 million from the already troubled city.

As caricatured by Thomas Nast with a corpulent body and vulpine face, Tweed became the symbol of dishonesty and public greed. He professed not to care: When reformers accused him of corruption, his response was a pleasant, "What are you going to do about it?"

For a long time, nobody did much of anything. Then in January of 1871, the city auditor was killed in a sleighing accident and was replaced by a man who was not under Tweed's thumb. The new auditor quietly amassed evidence of colossal municipal theft and turned it over to the New York *Times*. The trial that followed marked the end of the Tweed Ring. Although skeptics like George Templeton Strong were convinced that the "rank, old felonious dog-fox" would escape punishment, Tweed spent many of his last years in jail and died there in 1878.

It was Grant's misfortune that the Tweed scandal — as well as the news of the Credit Mobilier Affair — burst on the public on the eve of the 1872 presidential election campaign. The twin revelations lent force to an anti-Grant movement among Republicans who wanted a "new departure" for their party. Included among these self-styled Liberal Republicans were some of the most respected names in the party — Senator Charles Sumner, Congressman George W. Julian, and former Cabinet member Gideon Welles — along with a number of judges, lawyers, editors and intellectuals.

These men were as diverse and sometimes contradictory in their aims as they were in their backgrounds. Most of them subscribed to three broad goals: civil service reform, free trade and reconciliation between North and South. Beyond that, they were men with fiercely held and opposing beliefs about such issues as the gold standard, tariff protection, public corruption and the rights of blacks. But the idealists and the more practical power brokers among them agreed on one thing: The time had come to get rid of Grant, whom Senator Carl Schurz called the "great incubus pressing upon the party."

To do this was not going to be easy, for Grant was an immensely popular man. Even those who doubted his abilities as President felt a curious sympathy for him. After a meeting at the White House, James Russell Lowell wrote that he was struck by the touching look of Grant's face, "a puzzled pathos of a man with a problem before him which he does not understand." Nevertheless, Lowell added, "I liked Grant."

The Liberal Republicans clearly would need allies in order to unseat Grant, and the most obvious prospects were the Democrats. But ordinary differences aside, there were some former Radicals in the Liberal Republican ranks — George Julian, for example, and Charles Sumner; it seemed inconceivable that they could come to an agreement with the defenders of white supremacy.

As it turned out, the Democrats paved the way to an alliance. In May of 1871, former Congressman Clement Vallandigham, the

A campaign poster promotes Horace Greeley and his running mate, Benjamin G. Brown, who were nominated by the Democrats and the Liberal Republicans to challenge Grant for the presidency in 1872. Diarist George Templeton Strong reviled Greeley's nomination as "preposterous and ludicrous"; Greeley was honest, Strong said, but "so conceited, fussy, and foolish that he damages every cause he wants to support."

LIBERTY, EQUALITY AND FRATERNITY.

UNIVERSAL AMNESTY.

IMPARTIAL SUFFRAGE.

FOR PRESIDENT.

FOR VICE-PRESIDENT.

HORACE GREELEY AND BENJN. GRATZ BROWN

OF NEW YORK

OF MISSOURI

GRAND NATIONAL LIBERAL REPUBLICAN BANNER FOR 1872.

crat's national chairman, "is played out."

The way was thus opened for Liberal Republicans to talk of a coalition with the "better class of Democrats." But whom could these uneasy bedfellows nominate as a common opposition candidate? There was talk of drafting General Sherman. But he was definitely unacceptable to Democrats—and he made it abundantly clear that he was also unavailable: "What do you think I am, a damned fool?" Sherman demanded of Carl Schurz. "Look at Grant! Look at Grant! What wouldn't he give now if he had never meddled in politics!"

At the Liberal Party convention in Cincinnati in May of 1872, the favored candidates were the patrician former Ambassador Charles Francis Adams and millionaire Supreme Court Justice David Davis. The two front runners deadlocked, however, with virtually equal support, and on the fourth ballot an unexpected compromise winner emerged—the maverick newspaper editor and publisher Horace Greeley.

Few were completely satisfied with the choice. The 61-year-old Horace Greeley had made himself the leading Republican spokesman for amnesty, reconciliation and self-government in the South. But he was also regarded as both a tedious scold and an eccentric whose quackish views had alienated many people. In his *Tribune* columns, he had been a prominent and early antislavery spokesman, and a crusader for such diverse causes as land reform, the labor movement, vegetarianism and spiritualism. Never hobbled by consistency, Greeley had spoken as vehemently for total war as he had for a negotiated peace. He was on record at various times as being for a tough Reconstruction and for leniency toward former Confeder-

foremost pro-South Copperhead of the war years, proposed resolutions to a county Democratic convention in Ohio endorsing the 14th and 15th Amendments as "the natural and legitimate results of the War." Before the year was out, a dozen state Democratic conventions adopted the resolutions, and the more extreme racist rhetoric began to disappear from the speeches of the Democrats. "The game of charging us with disloyalty and Copperheadism," declared the Demo-

ates. He was "a queer old man," wrote Henry Watterson, the astute editor of the Louisville *Courier-Journal*, "a very medley of contradictions, shrewd and simple, credulous and penetrating." Following the Liberal Republicans' lead, the Democrats nominated Greeley in July. In June, the regular Republicans had nominated Grant for reelection without a dissenting vote.

Greeley's Liberal platform was a brief, uninspired document that betrayed the opposition's lack of a clear direction. Two of the planks dealing with the Southern question pledged "equal and exact justice to all of whatever nativity, race, color or persuasion." But other planks called for universal amnesty for ex-Confederates, withdrawal of Union troops and the restoration of "local self-government" — a euphemism widely understood to mean the restoration of white rule. Greeley endeavored to conceal the contradictions in the platform by appealing to what he sensed was a yearning for reconciliation. "Are we never to be done with this?" he asked. And replied: "The War is ended, let us again be fellow countrymen, and forget that we have been enemies."

It was a rough and one-sided campaign. The robber barons and the rest of the Eastern business community lined up solidly behind Grant, filling the coffers of the Republican Party. The veterans of the Grand Army of the Republic remained loyal to their General, and black voters held firm in their Republican allegiance. While Grant wisely remained silent — "I am no speaker and don't want to be beaten," he said — other Republican leaders indulged in political vilification and character assassination to a degree that stunned the unfortunate Greeley.

In the November voting, Greeley suffered a crushing defeat. Republicans carried every Northern state and 10 of the 16 Southern and border states as well, garnering a larger margin than they had in 1868. In addition to the presidency, Republicans regained an almost two-thirds majority in the House and preserved a similar edge in the Senate.

Three weeks after the election, an exhausted Greeley died of what was diagnosed as "brain fever." His funeral was attended by the President, the Vice President, members of the Cabinet and various governors. That gesture of reconciliation was significant, for it underscored a lesson of the campaign: Although the Liberal Republican movement died with Greeley, it had demonstrated that Democrats and Republicans had grown closer in their attitudes toward the South. Ostensibly, the election was a mandate for continuation of a tough Southern policy; in reality, it marked the beginning of a Republican movement away from Radical Reconstruction.

But scandals crowded even more thickly on one another in Grant's second term than they had in the first, seriously impairing his ability to govern. Although Grant himself was not involved in any dishonesty, he showed a myopic loyalty to friends and associates who were. This became clear in a delinquent-taxes scandal, which implicated Treasury Secretary William Richardson.

In what was supposed to be an effort to find and prosecute people who owed back taxes, Richardson hired an unsavory Boston ward heeler named John D. Sanborn as an informer. Sanborn claimed half of the money collected from every tax delinquent he denounced. In fact, he simply used Richardson's authorization to gain access to government files and then collected money the gov-

Ulysses S. Grant maintains a presidential demeanor in this painting made four years after he left office. Treasury Secretary George S. Boutwell observed that Grant craved not "the exercise of power" but "the possession of power as evidence of the public confidence."

# The Peaceful March of Sergeant Bates

ernment would have received anyway. In this fashion he made $213,500 in one year and put in for an additional $156,000 in expenses. Embarrassed by the ensuing Congressional investigation, Grant accepted Secretary Richardson's resignation — then appointed him to a federal judgeship.

The case angered many congressmen — as did the somewhat similar case of Secretary of War William W. Belknap, a former Union general who had fought under Grant at Vicksburg and had commanded one of Sherman's divisions during the March to the Sea.

A big, floridly handsome man with a beautiful and fashionable wife — his third — Belknap lived considerably beyond his means. He made up the difference by accepting $6,000 a year for delivering into the hands of a New York friend the lucrative Indian trading post at Fort Sill, in the Oklahoma Territory. Evidently, Belknap's second wife had arranged the payoff, and after her death he continued to accept the money. When the transgression came to light, and Congress threatened to impeach Belknap, Grant acted swiftly to secure his friend's resignation be-

On a spring day in 1868, citizens of Richmond flocked to the state capitol to welcome a traveler carrying the flag of the United States *(opposite)*. The man climbed to the capitol dome and, as cannon boomed and the onlookers cheered, he waved the Stars and Stripes over the former stronghold of the Confederacy.

The color-bearer was Sergeant Gilbert H. Bates, a Wisconsin farmer, Union veteran and man of strong political convictions. Unlike many Northerners, Bates felt that "the Southern people had resumed their affection for the flag and the Union." To prove it, he had walked with his flag from Vicksburg, Mississippi, with no escort, money or weapon. On his three-month, 1400-mile trek, much of it along the route of Sherman's march through Georgia and South Carolina, Bates reported that he and the flag met only "blessings and thanks and kindness."

In 1872 Bates marched again, this time in England from the Scottish border to London; he hoped to demonstrate that British hostility toward the Union, aroused by the wartime naval blockade, was a thing of the past. The warm reception Bates found in England *(below)* bore out his belief.

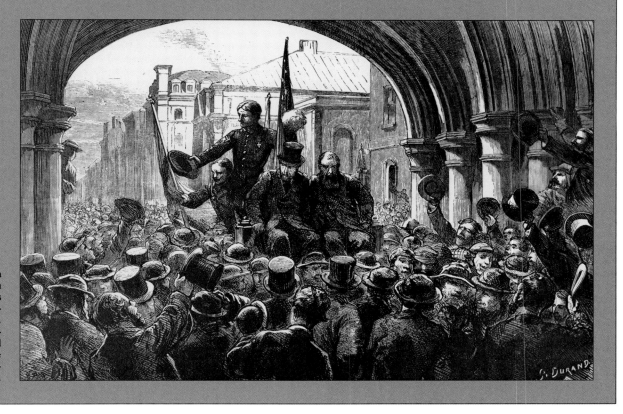

Sergeant Bates holds aloft the Stars and Stripes as he strides across the capitol grounds in Richmond in April of 1868. The flag was sewn for Bates by women in Vicksburg at the start of his march through the South.

Clutching the U.S. flag and a symbolic ball of American cotton, Sergeant Bates rides through London at the climax of his English journey. Some of the men in the welcoming crowd had unhitched his horses and claimed the privilege of drawing the carriage themselves.

fore the trial could begin, and the charges were dropped. Grant acted out of more than mere loyalty: His own brother Orvil had come into possession of four Indian posts through influence and had rented them out for a percentage of the profits.

But the most sensational scandal concerned the so-called Whiskey Ring, a conspiracy involving distillers, distributors and public officials who defrauded the government of millions in tax revenues. In essence, Treasury agents were bribed to overlook inaccurate measurements of bottled whiskey, or to issue tax stamps far in excess of the money paid for them. But the conspiracy spread beyond the government agents, to include important names in and out of government: Orville E. Babcock, the President's secretary; William McKee, editor of the St. Louis *Globe*; John A. McDonald, whom Grant had appointed collector of internal revenue west of the Mississippi. Babcock was not only a member of the President's official family but a personal friend; he had served Grant as aide-de-camp from The Wilderness to Appomattox.

The operations of the Whiskey Ring were uncovered by Benjamin Helm Bristow, an upright and ambitious Kentuckian, who had succeeded Richardson as Secretary of the Treasury. With the help of a reporter working covertly with the Treasury, Bristow determined that McDonald was the central figure in the conspiracy in the western region. Presented with the abundant evidence, Grant was cooperative at first. Following a raid on distillers and their cohorts in the Treasury Department, however, Grant grew uneasy. Bristow's persistent pursuit of Babcock and McDonald moved the President to tears. He began listening to advisers who told him that he was the real target of the investigation, and that Bristow was out to destroy the Republican Party.

McDonald was convicted and sent to prison despite the President's emphatic expression of sympathy for him. When Babcock's trial began, Grant did all he could to impede it. He agreed — and got his Cabinet to agree — to Babcock's request to be tried by a military court instead of a civilian jury. Babcock was acquitted by the army inquiry, but his trial was eventually returned to a criminal court at the insistence of a courageous district attorney in St. Louis, David P. Dyer.

Grant dispatched an investigator to St. Louis to obtain evidence exonerating Babcock, then fired the man when he came back with additional evidence of Babcock's guilt. Finally, the President took the unprecedented step of signing a deposition proclaiming his secretary's innocence. Read into the record at the trial, it procured Babcock's acquittal in February of 1876.

Grant intended to return Babcock to his post in the White House, but Secretary of State Hamilton Fish objected so strenuously

that the President abandoned the idea. Instead, he appointed Babcock superintendent of public buildings, a sinecure he held for several years before being drowned while inspecting a lighthouse in Florida. Bristow's reward for his diligence in breaking up the Whiskey Ring was to be pressured into resigning from the Cabinet.

The person who suffered most from the affair was the President himself. Aside from the continual distractions of dealing with his subordinates' trials and crises, Grant was increasingly regarded by the public as being unwilling or incapable of keeping his official house in order.

William W. Belknap, Grant's Secretary of War, resigned in 1876 after being charged with accepting bribes. Belknap later claimed that the mistake of his life was to resign "with the chivalric intention" of shielding his wife, who, Belknap said, had received the payoffs without his knowledge.

Postwar corruption was not restricted to the President's official family — or even to the industrial North. The South, too, was wracked by scandals that damaged the reputation of the Reconstruction governments and hampered the region's recovery. "Why, damn it, everybody is demoralizing down here," exploded Louisiana's carpetbag Governor Henry Clay Warmoth while testifying before a Congressional committee. "Corruption is the fashion."

Warmoth was well qualified to express such an opinion. Descended from a Virginia family that had migrated to Illinois, Warmoth liked to boast that he had "not a drop of any other than Southern blood" in his veins. He was said to have pocketed $100,000 in 1868, the first of his four years in office, while earning a salary of $8,000. He took payoffs for everything — the granting of charters and construction contracts, the allocation of school funds, the collection or noncollection of taxes.

Like other states under Radical Reconstruction governments, Louisiana under Governor Warmoth and his successor William P. Kellogg became notorious for fraudulent bond issues, graft in land sales and excesses in public spending. During the years of the Warmoth regime, the state spent an enormously inflated $1.5 million for public printing, much of the money going for kickbacks. Extravagant "expenses" that were paid to legislators made the cost of a Louisiana legislative session soar to almost 10 times what it had been before the War.

In this permissive and richly fraudulent society, the Louisiana Lottery flourished. The lottery's promoters gave it an air of scrupulous honesty by having two Confederate military heroes who had fallen on hard times, Pierre G. T. Beauregard and Jubal A. Early, preside at the public drawings. The company's share of the take was so great, however, that its owners became millionaires several times over; they prudently invested much of the profit they made in bribing the legislature to maintain their position as a state-chartered monopoly. Even the Chief Justice of Louisiana was involved in a fraudulent operation, in which a state-owned railroad was sold to political cronies for $50,000 after more than two million dollars had already been spent developing it.

Yet the prototype of the corrupt Southern government in the minds of most Northerners was not Louisiana but South Carolina. That state achieved its dubious reputation largely through the efforts of a militant Northern journalist named James Shepherd Pike. A former Maine politician, editor of Horace Greeley's New York *Tribune* and wartime Minister to the Netherlands, Pike was an opinionated man with deeply ambivalent feelings about blacks. As an early antislavery crusader he had insisted that "a great democratic republic cannot forever submit to the anomaly of Negro slavery in its bosom." But he felt just as strongly that blacks, "the ignorant and servile race," should not be raised to a position of equality with the "dominant and intelligent" whites.

In 1873, Pike visited South Carolina in order to observe its Reconstruction government. The lurid report he wrote — published initially as a series of newspaper articles and later as a book called *The Prostrate State* — had a profound influence on Northern thinking about the threatened "Africanization" of Southern states.

South Carolina at the time was atypical. Blacks dominated the legislature by a wide margin, 94 members out of 124, and were the dominant force in programs of social reform. Pike was at first somewhat sympathetic to the black legislators, conceding that they had "a genuine interest and a genuine earnestness in the business of the assembly which we are bound to recognize and respect." Gradually, however, he became dismayed at the sight of black legislators popping peanuts, munching plugs of tobacco and jabbering in "barbarous, animated jargon" about points of order and personal privilege without understanding either.

Pike saw evidence of corruption in the ornate new furnishings of the legislative chambers, in the rumor that $1,000 had been voted to the Speaker of the House as compensation to him for a losing bet on a horse, and in the legislative expense accounts that listed women's garters and chemises, whiskey, wine, perfume, Westphalia hams, gold watches and a metal coffin. Pike came to the conclusion that all of this and more was to be expected when power was taken out of the hands of "the remains of the old civilization" and given to "the ignorant, thiev-

ish, immoral, stupid, degraded black man."

In fact, it was white men who perpetrated the biggest frauds in the postwar South and made off with most of the spoils. No former slaves, for example, could equal the depredations of South Carolina's "robber governor," Franklin J. Moses Jr. And few blacks were involved in the most lucrative of all postwar swindles — the bribery of legislators to sell state-owned railroads to private companies at a fraction of their actual value. The schemes varied from state to state, but all were based on the assumption that bond is-sues could be inflated and, in the words of a later reform governor of South Carolina, "justice bought and sold."

Within the state capitols themselves, noted an Alabama editor wryly, "bribes were offered and accepted at noonday without hesitation or shame." A U.S. congressman visiting Columbia, South Carolina, was shocked to discover that bribery was practiced as a way of life by "even the old aristocratic class, to whom we have been taught to attribute sentiments of chivalric honor."

Nor did the situation improve when all-white Democratic administrations returned to power: After restoration of a "white supremacy government" in Mississippi, the Democratic state treasurer made off with $315,612 — more than the amount the Republicans had stolen in six years. The Democratic treasurers of Tennessee and Virginia would later disappear with $400,000 and $200,000, respectively. It was "a mortifying fact," lamented one Southern editor, that corruption "benefited about as many Democrats as Republicans."

Much of what seemed like graft was in fact simple inefficiency, and some of the reports of corruption were exaggerated to discredit the party involved. Emancipation had at a single stroke doubled the number of people requiring state services. In addition, the Reconstruction governments were attempting something new in American history: government largely by the poor, and dedicated at least in part to their interests. Saddled with many new social services, the Republican administrations were inevitably wasteful in carrying out programs for which they had no preparation. Public works employment, relief payments to the indigent, the rehabilitation of war-damaged properties —

In the engraving at left, former Confederate Generals P.G.T. Beauregard and Jubal Early preside at a drawing of the Louisiana state lottery in which slips from the glass-walled prize wheel (right) were matched with winning tickets drawn from a separate wheel. Granted a monopoly charter by the Louisiana legislature in 1868, the privately owned lottery soon had sales offices in every state, and reformers dubbed it "the Octopus."

all of these things cost enormous sums.

Expensive, too, was public education — an enterprise that soon embodied all of the hatreds and difficulties endemic to Reconstruction. In 1865, about 80 percent of Southern whites and 3 percent of blacks could read or write. When forced to provide education for blacks, each Southern state set up a separate school system for them. Alabama set aside one fifth of all its revenue for the support of public schools; Mississippi spent more for its public schools than for all other government activities combined.

Much of the cost of black education was at first borne by the Freedmen's Bureau and other benevolent societies, most of them church affiliated. The Freedmen's Bureau spent $16 million on black schools, while reaching only about 10 percent of the school-age black population. After 1871, the states began to take over support of both black and white schools, as provided by the new constitutions. But they did not dole out money to the two school systems equally. In Savannah, for instance, where black children outnumbered white, the school board in 1873 spent $64,000 on white schools, but the budget for blacks was a mere $3,000.

Militant white southerners deeply resented the black schools and often vented their anger on the teachers. At first, most of these teachers came from the North — the Freedmen's Bureau and various religious societies sent an estimated 5,000 of them into the South — but the balance gradually shifted after 1870 until the majority, both black and white, were recruited in the South. All of these educators faced ostracism and intimidation, and sometimes physical brutality. In Louisiana a black teacher was whipped, another stabbed and a third beaten to death as a warning to anyone planning what one of the assailants called "a damned nigger school." In Charleston, West Virginia, the Ku Klux Klan warned teachers in the "nig schools" to get out of town.

Those teachers who made it to their classrooms confronted a daunting task. A Northern teacher named Mary Ames was appalled by her first meeting with a class of South Carolina black children. "We opened school at nine o'clock with 15 scholars," she wrote. "Some were decently clad, others filthy and nearly naked," and none of them had ever been in a school before. When a large boy later told Mary Ames that he was three months old, she realized that the children were not only illiterate but unaware of their own ages. "We dismissed early," she wrote of her first day in class, "as the children seemed tired and we were decidedly weary."

When Laura M. Towne of Philadelphia opened a school in a South Carolina church, she was at first dismayed by the inability of her 80 pupils to respond: "They had no idea of sitting still, of giving attention, of ceasing to talk aloud," she recorded in her diary. "They lay down and went to sleep, they scuffled and struck each other. They evidently did not understand me, and I could not understand them, and after two hours and a half of effort I was thoroughly exhausted." Yet Laura Towne persevered — and in time she found gifted children such as "little Moses," a boy who had walked 200 miles to St. Helena's Island, South Carolina, from Wilmington, North Carolina, because there was no free school in Wilmington. Towne would spend nearly 40 years in the South, dedicating her life to the proposition that education should not be denied to what she called "the best and brightest" of either race.

Of the nine original Jubilee Singers (*left*), seven were born slaves. Ella Sheppard (*fourth from right*) had been bought out of slavery by her father and studied piano with a white teacher in Ohio — arriving for lessons through the back door, after dark.

A broadside announces an 1873 New York concert of the Jubilee Singers and explains the university building fund to which the proceeds will go. One listener said the singers "touched the font of tears, so that gray-haired men wept like children."

## "Slave Songs" That Saved a School

Among the more than 4,000 schools founded to educate blacks after the War was Nashville's Fisk University. When debt threatened to close the school in 1871, Fisk's treasurer and music teacher, George L. White, had a bold idea. Why not send the student chorus on a tour of the North to raise money?

That October, White and nine singers set out, as one of them said, "to sing the money out of the hearts and pockets of the people." The tour got off to a shaky start, offering such sentimental selections as "Home Sweet Home," and barely meeting expenses. But when the students ventured to sing some of their cherished "slave songs" — spirituals —

to a church conference in Ohio, the audience was thrilled. From there the Jubilee Singers progressed in triumph to New York, where influential churchman Henry Ward Beecher, assuring his flock that the group was no "Negro minstrel show," arranged concerts in the most prestigious churches. Another minister remarked that he had never seen his congregation "so moved and melted by the magnetism of music."

On subsequent tours over the next seven years, the Jubilee Singers took their "plantation hymns" all through the North and to Europe; they raised $150,000, and thus ensured the survival of their university.

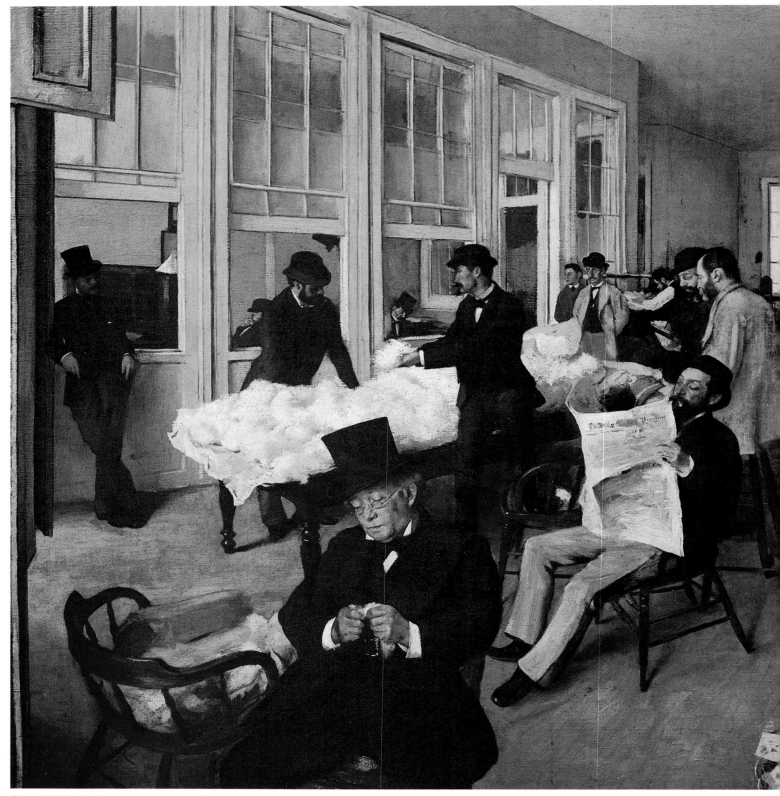

Cotton brokers judge new crop samples in this 1873 painting of a New Orleans trading firm, by the visiting French artist Edgar Degas. By 1880 Southern cotton

production exceeded prewar levels.

The efforts of teachers like Mary Ames and Laura Towne were not enough to educate the masses of blacks, but progress was made. By 1880, black illiteracy had been reduced to 75 percent. The white illiteracy rate remained basically unchanged in the same period. By 1876, more than half of school-age white children were in school and nearly two fifths of the black children were enrolled — a threefold increase in just six years. Southern universities were functioning again, and some two dozen black colleges and universities had opened their doors to provide higher education for what one black leader later called "the talented tenth."

This enormous educational effort, coupled with the other social responsibilities assumed by the Reconstruction governments, strained the already burdened Southern economy. Property taxes in many states were three times what they were in the more prosperous North. Sales taxes and poll taxes on every adult male became commonplace. The weight of such taxation had a depressing effect on the economy, which was far less healthy than it seemed to casual observers.

When the New York *Tribune's* Whitelaw Reid returned to the former Confederate states a year after seeing their postwar devastation, he was struck by "the rush of business" in streets that had once been deserted. In Mobile, Alabama, and later in Atlanta, he found "the 'new blood of the South' leaping in riotous pulsations." Reid's impression was shared by other Northerners visiting the Southern states, and in part it was borne out by figures. In the 15 years after the War, the number of Southern manufacturing establishments increased by 80 percent and the value of manufactured products by 55 percent. Not until 1878, however, did cotton production return to its prewar level. The rebuilt Southern railway system had expanded by only 7,000 miles compared with 45,000 miles of new track in the North.

The South, in fact, was being left in an economic backwash by the stunning growth of the more vigorous North. The South's railroad mileage had been 30 percent of the prewar national total; even after its postwar expansion it had dropped to 19 percent of the whole. During the same period, the Southern share of factories decreased from 14.7 percent to 11.5 percent of the national total. Per capita income in 1880 was only two fifths of what it was in the North — well below the two-thirds figure of prewar years.

An important reason for the South's economic malaise was the weakness of its agriculture. Although the number of farms doubled to well over a million between 1860 and 1880, ownership of the land was increasingly concentrated in the hands of a few. And they desperately needed labor.

After Appomattox, the majority of the freed slaves found themselves without an occupation. Having lost the dubious economic security of slavery, most blacks were forced to seek employment with their former masters, often working for wages that were minuscule by Northern standards. But bad crop yields in 1866 and 1867 so reduced the meager cash reserves of the plantation owners that they gradually adopted a share-crop or crop-lien system. The owner provided land, a dwelling, a team, seed and tools, and the cropper supplied the labor. At harvest, the owner usually received one half of the crop.

The system depended heavily on credit; the planter borrowed from a bank, his tenant farmer from the country storekeeper and the storekeeper from the city wholesaler. Black and white tenant farmers soon found themselves locked into the system by accumulated debt. The banker applied pressure on the landowner and the owner pressed the sharecropper to plant the most marketable cash crop, which was cotton.

The resulting overproduction not only exhausted the soil but made the South more dependent than ever on a one-crop economy. As cotton output rose, the price dropped by one half, forcing the cropper to plant yet more cotton to meet his debts. "It is cotton! cotton! cotton!" shrilled an embittered farmer in North Carolina. "Buy everything and make cotton pay for it." The cycle of debt and overproduction depressed the entire economy, contributing to a pervasive Southern impoverishment that helped keep wartime resentments alive.

In their quest for labor, the struggling planters and businessmen developed a new form of slavery known as convict leasing. Renting prisoners from the states' overcrowded prison systems provided the contractors with cheap labor and the states with welcome revenue. As the demand for convict labor increased, blacks were arrested on ever more petty charges such as vagrancy, fistfighting or carrying a weapon, and shipped off to chain gangs. There they were illfed, poorly clothed and brutally treated; the death rate among them ran as high as 50 percent in South Carolina.

Meanwhile the vicious system generated enormous fortunes for some: A planter named Edmund Richardson got control of almost all the convicts in Mississippi and became for a time the biggest cotton producer in the South; by dealing shrewdly in convicts, Alabama state warden John H. Bank-

head grew wealthy on a salary of $2,000 a year; Georgia's scalawag political boss Joseph Brown made his postwar fortune with convicts leased from the state for seven cents a day. In fact, so many powerful people profited from the system that it took reformers decades to end it.

Thus, the undernourished South and the overheated North lurched into the future, each afflicted by greed and corruption, each burdened in different ways by the awesome aftermath of four years of destruction. While the South wrestled with its social and economic devastation, the North sank ever deeper into the grip of debt.

Winning the War had been expensive; by 1863 it was costing $2.5 million a day. The government solved the problem temporarily by borrowing and by issuing a national currency called greenbacks. By the end of the War, more than two billion dollars in outstanding bonds threatened the nation's fiscal stability. In addition, the government had borrowed more than one billion dollars from other countries, and by 1866 the interest on this debt and other foreign payments was costing $130 million per year. In that same year, the public debt reached a postwar peak of $2.7 billion.

One result of the government's wartime spending had been a dizzying inflation. When Grant came into office in 1869, the more than $300 million in greenbacks still in use were worth only 73 cents on the dollar in gold. Grant opposed the immediate resumption of specie payment for domestic debts; he feared that making greenbacks redeemable in gold, dollar for dollar, would be unfair to debtors and would hurt business by tightening credit. Yet many men of influence in and out of the government felt that rampant speculation required just such a curb, and in February 1873, gold was made the country's sole monetary standard. At the same time, the Treasury began constricting the supply of paper currency.

As the summer of 1873 came to an end, the fiscal situation was rapidly worsening, but the high rollers in the financial citadels of the North were conducting business as usual — manipulating the stock market, building railroads, borrowing money far beyond their ability to repay and scrambling to lay their hands on any cash they could borrow. One of the titans was Jay Cooke, owner of Cooke and Company, the largest banking firm in the Western world. Cooke's loans to government and industry had financed much of the War and the postwar boom, and he felt the increasing pressure as much as any man, yet he continued to be confident. He wrote to his brother in mid-September that he retained "an unfailing confidence in the God in whom we put our trust: I do not believe He will desert us."

President Grant, on the other hand, saw that the frenzy could not continue; the country needed a rest, he observed, a "month of Sundays." What it got was far worse. On the evening of September 17, 1873, Grant was making an overnight visit to Jay Cooke's gloomy, granite mansion outside Philadelphia. Neither man was much given to conversation, and after dinner they sat in amicable silence, puffing on the private brand of cigars that Cooke kept in stock for the President. They evidently did not discuss the indications of severe strain on the investment market that had been troubling Wall Street for several days.

In the morning, Cooke shared a leisurely breakfast with the President, read some telegrams from his financial partner in New York, then suddenly excused himself, revealing nothing to the President. At his Philadelphia office, he confirmed the telegraphed report that the New York branch of Jay Cooke and Company had just closed its doors. In a desperate effort to finance construction of his Northern Pacific Railroad and keep money flowing to the railroad's work crews, Cooke had conceived a number of loan and equity arrangements that resulted ultimately in overextending his company. Weeping, Cooke ordered the Philadelphia office closed as well.

News of the gigantic banking firm's failure launched a panic whose effect would be felt for the rest of Grant's presidency and beyond. Within hours, other banks and commercial houses began shutting down; there was a run on the Union Trust Company, whose secretary fled New York with $250,000 of the firm's fast-shrinking capital. Leading stocks lost half their value, and two days later the New York Stock Exchange closed. Anxious speculators crowded the street in the rain, presenting "a compact mosaic of shiny umbrellas like a bed of mushrooms" to the observant George Templeton Strong. "The nation," said labor leader James Swank dryly, "is to have a period of enforced rest from industrial development."

The debacle was appalling: A quarter of the nation's railroads went into bankruptcy, more than 5,000 businesses failed in 1873 and commercial debt increased by $100 million. Forty percent of the nation's steel furnaces shut down.

Even more distressing was the misery and social disorder that followed. In Boston, a charity called the Overseers of the Poor re-

## A Triumph of Creative Diplomacy

The most vexing international problem, and ultimately the greatest diplomatic triumph, of Grant's presidency involved the rankling question of the *Alabama* claims. As early as 1862 the United States had demanded that Great Britain pay for damage inflicted by the C.S.S. *Alabama* and other Confederate warships built or fitted out in British ports. England acknowledged no liability; negotiations under Secretary of State Seward had foundered repeatedly.

Then in 1871, through the skillful efforts of Grant's Secretary of State Hamilton Fish, the two countries agreed to submit their dispute to arbitration — a solution that had no successful precedent. A five-nation tribunal meeting in Switzerland in 1872 decreed that England must pay the United States $15.5 million; for England's counterclaims, the U.S. must pay $1.9 million.

Both parties accepted the verdict, and a decade-old irritant was removed. "The great experiment," said a U.S. participant, "has been carried to a successful end."

An engraving from a popular songsheet commemorates the 1864 sea battle in which the U.S.S. *Kearsarge (near right)* sank the famed commerce raider C.S.S. *Alabama* in the English Channel. The British yacht *Deerhound (center)* helped rescue the Confederate crew.

ported a dangerous doubling up in already overcrowded tenements. Elsewhere, the perennial vagrant population was joined by large numbers of desperate men wandering the roads in search of jobs. The unemployed — who numbered about a million at the worst of the crisis — depended for their survival on soup kitchens set up by private relief organizations.

Theft and violent crime became so widespread that isolated houses in some regions were abandoned for fear of attack. A gang of vagrants took over and terrorized the town of Jacksonville, Illinois; another group of 200 vagrants in the same state seized a train outside Beardstown, ran it into town and fought a battle with the marshal and his deputies.

It would be several years before the staggering economy regained its health. But by the end of the decade industrial production was expanding at a sedate pace, the stock market was functioning again and the lines of the unemployed had gradually disappeared from the streets.

The more enduring effect of the Panic was to push the problems of Reconstruction even lower on the list of national priorities. Southern propaganda emphasizing the corruption of the Reconstruction governments had something to do with this. Moreover, Northern voters had grown weary of what a Republican politician called the "worn-out cry of 'Southern outrages.'"

There were other influences at work, too. The War, along with the fervent emotions it engendered, was receding into the past. "There are a vast number of Republicans," noted Carl Schurz, "who have lost their fear of the return of the Rebellion to power." Northern businessmen actually desired an end to Reconstruction; they were beginning to believe that the Republican carpetbag governments were the chief impediments to economic development of the South. It was time to get out of Southern politics entirely, they argued, and turn the so-called "black question" over to the Southerners themselves to resolve.

At the same time an odd kind of sympathy for Southerners was growing in the minds of Northern reformers. The old, genteel Yankee families from whom much of the abolitionist fervor had come were beginning to feel insecure in postwar America. Their power had been eroded by the rapid rise of new industrial wealth, and they felt menaced by the flood of immigrants that was changing the face of American cities.

While strolling on the Boston Common one Sunday afternoon, the author Henry James found himself confronted by hordes of people among whom "no sound of English" could be heard: "The greater number spoke a rude form of Italian, the others some out-land dialect unknown to me. The types and faces bore them out; the people before me were gross aliens to a man, and they were in serene and triumphant possession." Thus beleaguered, established families such as the Jameses began to feel a stirring of empathy for the whites living among the blacks of the South. The "best classes at the North," wrote abolitionist leader William French, now regarded white Southerners as "a kindred people."

There was also a feeling of disappointment in the North with the use blacks had made of their freedom. James Pike's *The Prostrate State* had helped spread the notion of black ineptitude and corruption, and the suspicion was now growing that blacks could not govern themselves. Edwin L. Godkin, editor of *The Nation*, was typical of the liberal thinkers who had expected a swift transformation of the black population as soon as the bonds of slavery were removed. When this did not occur, Godkin became disillusioned. The experiment in black, carpetbagger government, he proclaimed, had totally failed: "We owe it to human nature to say that worse governments have seldom been seen in a civilized country." Echoing these sentiments, Carl Schurz gave a speech in which he sadly but firmly abandoned the cause of Reconstruction.

In the Congressional elections of November 1874, the Democrats won a 60-seat majority in the House. The elections had many meanings, but the one the South chose to see most clearly was that Northern support for Reconstruction was rapidly waning. The way was now prepared for white Southerners to attempt a major assault on the Reconstruction governments from within.

# A Crusader with Pen and Ink

THOMAS NAST IN 1866

As General Robert E. Lee and his fellow Confederates beg forgiveness, a brooding Columbia — Nast's female personification of a united America — ponders whether to trust the repentant Rebels. The cartoonist sided with the Radical Republicans in demanding harsh and unforgiving treatment of the South and its leaders.

PARDON

Columbia — "SHALL I TRUST THESE MEN,

FRANCHISE

AND NOT THIS MAN?"

No one ever accused cartoonist Thomas Nast of objectivity. From 1865 until 1884, Nast's acerbic drawings chronicled the burning issues of Reconstruction politics with a partisan zeal that could make — or break — the most powerful of men. "I try to hit the enemy between the eyes," said Nast, "and knock him down."

Nast's barbs brought down the graft-ridden New York City machine of William "Boss" Tweed. His biting satire doomed the presidential hopes of Horace Greeley. And his contempt for Andrew Johnson inspired a distinctive style of caricature (*following pages*) that evolved from his more realistic early work, shown here as it appeared in the influential *Harper's Weekly*.

Nast's impact resulted largely from his genius for reducing complex issues to simple but compelling images. His attention to detail was also prodigious: His crowd scenes, for example, typically contain scores of recognizable public figures. And the targets of his wrath remained instantly identifiable even as Nast exaggerated without mercy their physical and intellectual eccentricities.

Nast's fertile imagination produced several enduring national symbols, including the modern conceptions of Columbia *(left)* and Uncle Sam. Perhaps his most famous legacy, however, is his incarnation of American political parties as the Democratic donkey and the Republican elephant.

A solicitous Columbia, her hand on the shoulder of a one-legged black veteran, asks why he is still denied the basic rights of citizenship. Nast's commitment to racial equality was evident in his deliberate juxtaposition of the black war hero with contrite Confederates *(opposite)* in the August 5, 1865, issue of *Harper's Weekly*.

AMPHITHEATRUM JOHNSONIANUM — MASSACRE OF THE INNOCENTS AT NEW ORLEANS, July 30, 1866.

With the arrogance of Caesar at a Roman spectacle, President Johnson (*seated*) and his Cabinet preside over the slaughter of helpless civilians by police carrying a Confederate standard. The panorama was inspired by a riot in New Orleans in July 1866, during which white police fired on predominantly black participants in a political meeting. Nast, who blamed the bloodshed on Johnson's tolerance of Southern racism, suggests future trouble for the imperious President: At lower left, General Philip Sheridan, with sword drawn, has to be restrained by a less impetuous fellow-conspirator, General Ulysses S. Grant.

# At War with Corruption

William Marcy Tweed learned to his chagrin that Thomas Nast was one opponent who could not be bought. Rebuffing bribes amounting to half a million dollars, Nast waged graphic war on the New York political boss in the pages of *Harper's Weekly*, exposing the hypocrisy with which Tweed pillaged the city while posing as a champion of its poor.

Nast's courageous campaign brought nation-wide fame to the young cartoonist and tripled *Harper's* circulation. "My constituents don't know how to read," lamented Tweed, "but they can't help seeing them damned pictures." Ultimately, an aroused public sent Tweed and several of his cohorts to prison.

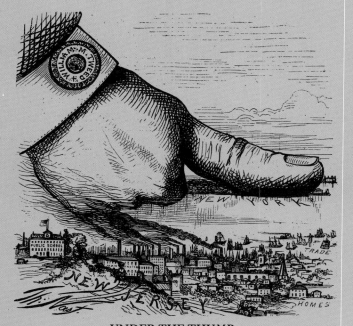

UNDER THE THUMB.
The Boss — "Well, what are you going to do about it?"

In answer to Tweed's defiant "what are you going to do about it?" challenge to reformers, Nast launched a relentless clean-up campaign with this 1871 cartoon showing New York under the corrupt politician's thumb. Nast's memorable caricatures helped put Tweed in jail. When he escaped and fled to Spain, the Spanish police captured him with the aid of a Nast drawing.

While New York's working families find the city treasury empty (*below, left*), Tweed and his cronies feast on their ill-gotten gains. Through bill-padding, kickbacks and outright theft, Tweed's graft ring looted almost $200 million of public funds in less than a decade.

EMPTY TO THE WORKMEN.

THE FOUR MASTERS THAT EMPTIED IT.

THE CITY TREASURY.

A GROUP OF VULTURES WAITING FOR THE STORM TO "BLOW OVER." — "LET US *PREY*."

## Assault on a Wayward Republican

For Republican purists such as Thomas Nast, presidential candidate Horace Greeley's 1872 alliance with the Democrats reeked of crass political expediency. Nast, a partisan of President Grant, attacked Greeley with a vehemence that led the former editor to wonder whether he was running for "the White House or the penitentiary."

Nast's anti-Greeley cartoons combined graphic ingenuity with devastating visual puns. After Greeley promised that his newspaper, the *Tribune* would not serve as a "party organ," Nast drew Greeley's successor as an organ grinder. And when Nast could not find a picture of Greeley's running mate, Benjamin Gratz Brown, he introduced the hapless Brown as a nametag pinned to Greeley's coattail.

"WHAT ARE YOU GOING TO DO ABOUT IT,"
IF "OLD HONESTY" LETS HIM LOOSE AGAIN?

Camouflaging the corruption of his Democratic allies, presidential candidate Greeley (*above*) whitewashes the Tammany Tiger, symbol of New York's supposedly reformed Democratic machine. Uncle Sam looks on in dismay at this betrayal of Republican principles.

Mocking the opportunism of the Liberal Republican alliance with antiblack Democrats, Nast pictures Greeley and his supporter Senator Charles Sumner exhorting a freedman to shake hands with his family's killers, a bloody Klansman and a gun-toting New York Irishman.

IT IS ONLY A TRUCE TO REGAIN POWER ("PLAYING POSSUM").
H. G. "Clasp hands over the bloody chasm."
C. S. "Freely accept the hand that is offered, and reach forth thine own in friendly grasp."

Going down to ignominious defeat, Horace Greeley falls into a political purgatory populated by squabbling allies and littered with the mastheads of supportive newspapers. Overhead, a beaming Uncle Sam congratulates President Grant on his landslide reelection.

CLASPING HANDS OVER THE BLOODLESS (SAR)C(H)ASM.

# A Bestial Defense of the President

Early in 1875, President Grant intervened in a controversial election for governor of Louisiana, throwing his support — and the backing of federal troops — to the Republican candidate. The ensuing storm of controversy, led by strong criticism in New York's leading newspapers, whetted the partisan talents of Thomas Nast.

Taking a cue from his editor's complaint that "there has been rather too much bayonet," Nast used a well-known journalistic hoax of the day to humble Grant's detractors. A year earlier, one of the same journalists who now berated the President had set off a public panic with a phony story describing a mass escape of wild animals from New York's Central Park Zoo. In its current criticism, suggested Nast's cartoon, the press was again trafficking in trumped-up sensationalism.

A ferocious-looking menagerie of bayonet-headed birds and beasts rushes out of a "zoological arsenal" in this 1875 cartoon, in which Nast lampoons press criticism of President Grant for being too precipitous in his use of military force. In contrapuntal insets, Nast shows a lionlike Grant force feeding the facts to Democratic donkeys (*upper right*) and slaying the serpents of a rumor-mongering press with a dagger of truth.

THE BIGGEST SCARE AND HOAX YET! — THE WILD ANIMALS LET LOOSE AGAIN BY THE ZOOMORPHISM PRESS.

# Learning to Live with Compromise

The postwar reign of Radical Republicanism that had inspired Thomas Nast's artistic imagination ended with the 1877 inauguration of President Rutherford B. Hayes. As the moderate, compromise candidate of a more conciliatory Republican Party, Hayes won a hairbreadth victory over a Democratic opponent whose policies were often indistinguishable from his own.

Nast's work responded to the country's new mood with a broadened political perspective and moments of self-criticism (*below*). For the first time, the elephant and the donkey appear together (*opposite*). The juxtaposition was appropriate: The issue of sound money, once a litmus test of Radical Republicanism, was now being championed by a responsible Democrat.

"NAY, PATIENCE, OR WE BREAK THE SINEWS." — SHAKESPEARE.
U.S.: "Our Artist must keep cool, and sit down, and see how it works."

Still an unregenerate Radical, Nast is restrained by a tolerant Uncle Sam in this 1877 self-caricature. Nast's unhappiness with the conciliatory Southern policies of newly inaugurated President Rutherford B. Hayes was tempered by his realization that the national mood was shifting from wartime partisanship toward compromise and reconciliation.

Democratic Senator Thomas Bayard, an advocate of a sound money policy, pulls his party's donkey back onto solid financial ground while a self-satisfied Republican elephant slumbers nearby. By reducing a complex controversy to these vivid images, Nast captured the narrowing differences separating Republicans and Democrats in the late 1870s.

STRANGER THINGS HAVE HAPPENED.

HOLD ON, AND YOU MAY WALK OVER THE SLUGGISH ANIMAL UP THERE YET.

# Retreat from Reconstruction

*"We have got rid of nothing by the War but slavery and the faith in the possibility of secession by which the South was pervaded. We have not got rid of the imperfection of the moral perceptions — of the hard, coarse love of gain — of the caste pride and of race prejudice which made slavery possible."*

THE NATION, JANUARY 30, 1868

In the spring of 1876, a prominent Louisiana businessman, politician and carpetbagger named Marshall Harvey Twitchell boarded a ferry across the Red River from his adopted home of Coushatta. As the skiff carried Twitchell and his brother-in-law toward the town, they noticed a man pacing the high bank at the river's edge. He was wearing an ankle-length rubber coat, a false beard, eye goggles and a slouch hat pulled over his face.

When the ferry touched the bank, the stranger drew a Winchester repeater from under his coat and fired. "Down in the boat!" shouted Twitchell. His brother-in-law got off one shot with a pistol, then died with a bullet in his head. Twitchell, wounded in the leg, jumped into the water and ducked under the skiff, clutching the edge of the boat. The stranger kept firing, steadily and accurately, hitting and breaking one of Twitchell's arms, then the other. The black ferryman, despite his terror, grabbed Twitchell's collar to keep him afloat.

A crowd began to gather, not comprehending at first what was happening. Some thought that the cool gunman was firing at an animal in the river. One man tried to approach; the gunman swung the rifle on him, snarling, "God damn you, go back!" The man retreated. A woman, seeing that there was a dead man in the boat and a wounded man in the water, pleaded with the gunman to stop firing. Ignoring her, he emptied his rifle and then started shooting deliberately with a pistol. A bullet smashed the ferryman's hand. Howling in anguish, he yelled that the man in the water was dead. At that the gunman calmly put his pistol into its holster, walked to his horse and started to ride away. Somebody asked him if he had been shooting at an alligator. "Yes," said the gunman. "It is a damned black alligator."

Twitchell was not black, but he was a friend of blacks. Somehow he survived his six bullet wounds and the amputation of both arms, to tell his story to an investigating committee of the 44th Congress. His harrowing experiences in postwar Louisiana, which came to a bloody climax at the Coushatta ferry that day, mirrored in many ways the rising tide of Southern rage and the deterioration of the Reconstruction governments the South despised.

A veteran of the 4th Vermont Infantry, Twitchell had become an agent of the Freedmen's Bureau at the War's end and was assigned to the village of Sparta, Louisiana. Before long, he married the daughter of a prominent local family, then took over the management of the family's estates and became involved in Radical Republican politics. He was a member of the state's constitutional convention and subsequently became a justice of the peace, assistant marshal, state senator and United States commissioner. He felt for a while that he had been accepted by his new neighbors.

Then, in the spring of 1868, the night rid-

This uniform blouse was worn by a member of the South Carolina Red Shirts, a paramilitary group that worked relentlessly to return white Democrats to public office. Upon joining the Red Shirts, an initiate pledged to "control the vote of at least one Negro, by intimidation, purchase, or keeping him away" from the polls.

ers began to appear. They shot and beheaded a local black leader named Moses Langhorne; they wounded Twitchell's neighbor and fellow carpetbagger with shotguns. When they came to call on him one night, Twitchell slipped out the back door, barely escaping with his life. From then on, Twitchell, his family and friends lived in constant danger. His mulatto messenger disappeared: People said the youth had been attacked by mounted men, bound and thrown into nearby Lake Bistineau. One Sunday the local minister devoted his sermon to an attack on Twitchell's wife for marrying an outsider. Worried, Twitchell rode only in daylight in open country, never near woods, and he feared for his family's safety. But he was also tough and proud: In 1868, he cast the only vote for Grant recorded in the entire parish.

Despite the harassment, Twitchell prospered. On 620 acres of the best land in the Red River valley, he set up a steam-powered cotton gin, a saw mill and a grist mill in a thriving complex that he ran with the help of his in-laws and of relatives from Vermont. These enterprises brought new economic life to the valley and changed Coushatta from a sleepy hamlet into a busy commercial center. He built houses for black workers, contributed money for churches and public buildings, dredged Lake Bistineau for navigation and gave the parish its first public schools.

Twitchell also accumulated political power. He became chairman of the state senate finance committee and the leading political boss of Red River parish. Although he derived most of his political support from blacks — they constituted 70 percent of the local population — he was also popular among white merchants who were doing more business than they ever had before.

Yet the hatred, and the potential for violence, was always present. In April of 1873, in the neighboring town of Colfax, one of the worst antiblack riots in the Reconstruction era occurred. Louisiana was still disputing the 1872 election results; both candidates for governor claimed victory. In Colfax, each would-be governor had appointed supporters as parish judge and sheriff. These claims led to a clash between Radical Republicans and white conservatives, in which black deputies exchanged gunfire with whites.

The black population of the surrounding countryside, fearing retaliation, flocked into Colfax, entrenched in front of the courthouse and awaited attack. In the unequal battle that followed, a white mob killed 105 blacks while suffering only three fatalities. Some of the defenders were shot down behind their breastworks, some were burned to death when the whites set fire to the courthouse, and others were murdered after they surrendered. The New Orleans *Times* recounted the massacre under the exultant headline, "War at Last!!" Somebody wrote Twitchell and told him he had better flee: The whites responsible for the Colfax massacre were coming to Coushatta "to kill all the yankees and Nigger officers." Twitchell announced that force would be met by force, and the marauders held off.

Nevertheless, the strain of operating in a

hostile environment was beginning to tell on Twitchell. People he had counted as friends started avoiding him. While he was in New Orleans in August of 1874, a mob descended on Coushatta, killed several blacks and made a prisoner of virtually every white Republican leader in the parish. Three days later, six of the captive Republicans were murdered, including Twitchell's brother and two of his brothers-in-law. After that, reported the federal commander in the district, "scarcely a Negro dared to sleep in his home."

In October, Twitchell returned to Coushatta with an army escort, but he could not be protected for long. He began to resettle what remained of his family in Vermont, and after the ambush on the Red River that nearly killed him, he left Louisiana, once again under heavy guard. The white South's animosity was too strong, he sadly admitted. Not surprisingly, he was no longer sure that "right would finally prevail."

Twitchell's experiences were far from unique. By the mid-1870s, the Republican Party in the South had lost its confidence in the face of a tide of violence that the federal government seemed powerless to control. President Grant had declared in 1874 that he had "no desire to have United States troops interfere in the domestic concerns of Louisiana or any other State." Grant believed it better to let matters take their course, even at the expense of black liberties, than to embroil the federal government, perhaps irreversibly, in a race war.

The politically divided Congress was becoming similarly disinterested, apparently preferring not to see what was going on. This attitude persisted even after the day in June of 1876 when Marshall Twitchell was carried on a litter before a touring committee of the House. He talked long and eloquently of what had happened to him, and what was happening to Louisiana. But the committee dodged the issue by deciding that the Coushatta Affair had not been politically motivated, and thus was not a federal concern.

The neglect had begun long before that, and in Louisiana as in other Southern states, militant whites were emboldened by the lenient attitude of the federal government. They organized new paramilitary groups, especially after federal attorneys dropped virtually all charges against suspected members of the Ku Klux Klan in 1874. The ostensible aim of these so-called Rifle Clubs, White Leagues, Red Shirts and the like was to maintain public order; their real mission was the destruction of Republican governments and the banishment of blacks from public life. Unlike the Klan, they drilled and paraded openly — indeed, they wanted to attract the attention of blacks to their activities. In open mockery of federal attempts to curb them, vigilante groups in South Carolina called themselves "mounted baseball clubs," or "musical clubs."

The most influential of these groups emerged in Opelousas, Louisiana, in April of 1874. Inspired by a racist newspaper called the *Caucasian*, a number of whites formed what they called a White League, dedicated to the preservation of a "white man's government" and the suppression of "the insolent and barbarous African." They would not incite bloodshed, said the White Leaguers, but "if a single hostile gun is fired between the whites and blacks, every carpetbagger and scalawag that can be caught will in twelve hours be hanging from a limb." Within months of the meeting in Opelousas, White Leagues had spread throughout the South.

New Orleans police, on orders from Republican Governor William Kellogg, break up a meeting of Democrat John McEnery's state legislature in 1873. Both Kellogg and McEnery had claimed victory in the 1872 election, and President Grant recognized Kellogg, while lamenting that "the muddle down there is almost beyond my fathoming."

By the fall of 1874, the White Leagues of Louisiana alone had enrolled 14,000 members, most of them Confederate veterans. Opposed to this force were 130 federal troops, divided among three widely separated garrisons. Eyeing the disproportionate forces, a White Leaguer predicted that the Republicans would be out and the Democrats "in control of the Gov't within six months." Republican Governor William P. Kellogg agreed: In a series of increasingly desperate telegrams, he pleaded for federal aid. Already White Leaguers were in control of the countryside, and arms were pouring into New Orleans from outside the state.

The massacre of Republican officials at Coushatta on August 30, 1874, finally goaded Grant into action. On September 5, he ordered the 3rd Infantry Regiment to Louisiana from Mississippi. But the transfer was carried out slowly — in part because railway officials sympathetic to the Democrats delayed the troop trains. Meanwhile, the word went out to New Orleans whites to meet near the statue of Henry Clay on September 14 and "declare that you mean to be free."

When Governor Kellogg was told that 5,000 armed men had assembled to demand his resignation, he took refuge in the Customs House, declaring he would not quit. In the resultant bloody showdown, White Leaguers routed a force of 3,500 black militiamen and city police led by former Confederate General James Longstreet. Within an hour, the Kellogg government had fallen.

For three days New Orleans and the government of Louisiana were in the hands of a white supremacist mob, operating in defiance of federal authority. At last Grant moved decisively, ordering six more infantry companies into Louisiana to restore order and Republican rule. Under their protection, Kellogg returned to power.

But the troubles were far from over. "The State government has no power outside the United States Army," warned Major Lewis Merrill, commander of the Upper Red River District. "The White League is the only power in the State."

In the fall state elections, the Democrats won a majority in the lower house of the legislature. But a Republican review board

threw out the results from several parishes because blacks had been too afraid to vote. And the Republicans later physically ejected five Democratic legislators from the house with the aid of federal troops, thus reaffirming Republican rule at bayonet point. General Philip Sheridan, back in Louisiana at Grant's request, further angered Louisiana Democrats by recommending that the "banditti" leaders of the White Leagues should be arrested and tried by military courts.

"I have repeatedly and earnestly entreated the people of the South to live together in peace," Grant told Congress—and there is no question he was sincere. But reaction to his actions in Louisiana demonstrated how limited his political options were. Although many Republicans applauded the President's stand, others bitterly criticized the army's invasion of a legislature. "If this can be done in Louisiana," said Carl Schurz, who had been elected to the Senate from Missouri, "how long will it be before it can be done in Massachusetts and Ohio? How long before a soldier may stalk into the national House of Representatives, and, pointing to the Speaker's mace, say, 'Take away that bauble!' "

Even among those who backed Grant's actions, there was little support for a purely military solution to Louisiana's problems. Democratic unruliness in the South may have alienated Northern opinion, but it also increased the North's weariness with Southern affairs. In an attempt to bring at least temporary peace to Louisiana, Congress imposed a compromise solution in which the Democrats were allowed to retain control of the lower house in return for a pledge not to interfere with Governor Kellogg during his remaining two years in office.

Louisiana's situation was typical of the

144

Among the Confederate leaders who returned to politics after Congress restored their right to hold public office were former Generals John B. Gordon (*far left*) and Wade Hampton (*near left*) and diplomat Lucius Q. C. Lamar (*center*). All three men served in Congress, and Lamar later became a Justice of the Supreme Court.

rest of the South. In state after state, violence flared as whites set out to bring down the Reconstruction governments by force and intimidation. Their efforts at subversion were aided by the Congressional Amnesty Act of May 1872, which restored the right of holding office to almost all the Southern leaders who had been barred by the 14th Amendment. Familiar ex-Confederates such as Georgia's Alexander Stephens and Mississippi's Lucius Quintus Cincinnatus Lamar now returned to Congress. At the state level, there was a rush back into politics by some of the most diehard white supremacists.

In Alabama during the election campaign of 1874, the newly confident white leadership executed a well orchestrated series of maneuvers. These included multiple voting for Democratic candidates; blacklisting, intimidation and dismissal of black employees who supported Republicans; and massive intrusion at Republican meetings to harass the speakers. "You might as well quit," a black Republican campaign worker was warned. "We will carry the state or kill half of you on election day." The state went Democratic by a comfortable margin.

Mississippi whites, heartened by what had happened in Alabama, adopted the same tactics in their own state elections in 1875. The so-called Shotgun or Mississippi Plan, under the direction of a former Confederate officer named J. Z. George, soon became the model for militant action throughout the South.

Mississippi Democrats drew what they called the "white line," which in effect meant that any white man not enrolled in a Democratic club was subjected to ostracism, economic reprisals or worse. They applied so much pressure to the few remaining scalawags and carpetbaggers that these unfortu-

nates had little choice but to renounce their Republican allegiance or leave the state.

In some towns, armed men walked menacingly behind leading Republicans whenever they appeared in public. At night, Republican politicians and their families were awakened by the sound of gunfire. When Colonel James Lusk, a prominent white Republican in Mississippi, explained to his black supporters why he must leave the party, he spoke for all Southern whites who supported the politics of Reconstruction: "No white man can live in the South in the future and act with any other than the Democratic party unless he is willing and prepared to live a life of social isolation and remain in political oblivion. I am compelled to choose." The choice for most was clear, and white Republicans by the hundreds changed sides.

One who did not defect was Mississippi Governor Adelbert Ames, an incorruptible former Union general from Maine — a hero of Bull Run and Gettysburg — who hoped to remake Mississippi in the model of New England. Ames managed to overcome his aversion to the South — "Slavery blighted this people," he wrote gloomily to his wife. At the same time, Ames regarded his fellow carpetbaggers as "an audacious, pushing crowd" who were out to loot the state, and he grew disillusioned by the ignorance and corruption among the blacks he worked with. He was also appalled by the racial violence that seemed steadily to mount.

A favorite White-Liner terror tactic was the incited riot: Whenever Republicans gathered, armed whites would provoke an incident and open fire. In one of the worst of these incidents, before a local election at Vicksburg in December of 1874, at least 35 blacks and two whites were gunned down. In

# The Invisible Empire's Campaign of Terror

The Confederate veterans who rushed to join the Ku Klux Klan in the postwar South had come home to wrenching change. Disarmed, disenfranchised and dispossessed, they were appalled at the freedman's gun, his vote and his "going about at night." Reviving the tradition of slave patrols, by which white men for 170 years had kept blacks in check, the night-riding Klan sprang up, as one member put it, "to preserve society."

Calling their organization the "Invisible Empire," the Klansmen mounted a war of terror to disarm and control or kill blacks and their Reconstruction allies. State and federal laws against Klan activity, and Grand Wizard Nathan Bedford Forrest's half-hearted order in 1869 that the Klan disband, failed to end the violence. Even after Southern governments were firmly back in white control, the KKK persisted.

Two federal officers model Klan garb confiscated in Alabama in 1868. Klansmen intimidated their victims by saying they were the ghosts of dead Confederates, visiting from hell.

The ceremonial Grand Banner of the Klan in Maury County, Tennessee, typifies the KKK's fanciful, baleful trappings. The Latin motto means, "What always, what everywhere, what by all" is held to be true.

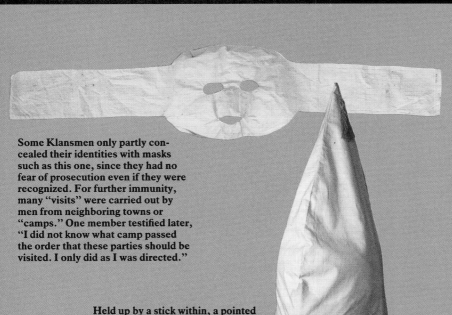

Some Klansmen only partly concealed their identities with masks such as this one, since they had no fear of prosecution even if they were recognized. For further immunity, many "visits" were carried out by men from neighboring towns or "camps." One member testified later, "I did not know what camp passed the order that these parties should be visited. I only did as I was directed."

Held up by a stick within, a pointed hood such as this gave Klansmen the desired ghostly look, but some of them added hair, quills and red paint for increased menace. Many of their shroudlike robes were sewn by women who found materials and instructions tossed through their windows, and who made the costumes without knowing the owners' names.

This miniature coffin was left on the doorstep of a black or a carpetbagger as notice of the Klan's sinister intentions. An accompanying note often included the warning, "Some live today — tomorrow die."

rural areas, blacks suspected of Republican sympathies were routinely murdered. An elderly black named Charles Green was ordered to cook a meal for a mob of 100 whites and was then shot by a white man, who explained that he wanted to try out his gun. A black farmer recalled that after whites fired into a black crowd at a Republican barbecue, killing two women and four children, the attackers moved out into the countryside to "hunt the whole country clean out," stalking and shooting fleeing blacks in the woods "just the same as birds."

As part of their campaign of terror, White Liners set up dummy targets representing blacks, riddled them with bullets in shooting contests, then paraded the battered dummies through Mississippi towns. In the capital of Jackson, reported Governor Ames's wife, "the crack of the pistol or gun is as frequent as the barking of the dogs."

After federal help was refused — "The whole public are tired out with these annual autumnal outbreaks in the South," wired Grant's attorney general — Ames recruited a black militia company. Alarmed, the White Liners promised not to disrupt the election if Ames disbanded the militia; when he complied they resumed the violence.

Ames denounced the federal government for remaining inactive while "a revolution has taken place, and a race are disenfranchised." The blacks, he predicted, were condemned to a second era of slavery. But he was too weary to carry the fight any further: "No matter if they are going to carry the State — let them carry it, and let us be at peace and have no more killing."

On election day, armed whites turned blacks away from the polls while voting repeatedly themselves. In the town of Aberdeen, White Liners kept a cannon loaded with chains and slugs trained on the voting place while the terrified Republican sheriff locked himself in his own jail. Any blacks brave enough to approach the ballot boxes were surrounded and beaten. The Democrats won handily, of course, in an election distinctive for many reversals of voting form; in Yazoo County, for example, where there had been a racial massacre, seven Republican votes were recorded in this election, compared to 2,500 in the previous one.

Mississippi White Liners obliterated the Republican majority of 30,000 votes of two years earlier and replaced it with a Democratic majority of 30,000. Nor did the violence end. With the election over and the threat of federal intervention past, the White Liners settled some political scores — most notably, black state Senator Charles Caldwell's being shot by whites in a Clinton tavern. When Caldwell asked to die in the open air, his assailants carried him into the street and shot him 30 times more.

When the newly elected Democratic legislators convened in 1876, they began impeachment proceedings against Governor Ames, who resigned rather than face a stacked political vote. With Mississippi back under white supremacist rule, the Meridian *Mercury* made a grim prediction: "The Negro, in these States, will be a slave again or cease to be. His sole refuge from extinction will be in slavery to the white man."

By 1876, only Louisiana, South Carolina and Florida still had Republican governments. All the other Southern states had been "redeemed" — as the white supremacists referred to their resumption of control. The Republican losses, along with the national Depression set off by the Panic of 1873, and the scandals of the Grant administration, had weakened the party as it prepared for the presidential election of 1876.

More was at stake than the name of the next President. Obviously, the fate of Reconstruction was about to be decided. Then too, Republican business interests feared that a resurgent South might ally itself with the agrarian West, as it had in the past, and undermine the wartime legislation responsible for much of the industrial boom. The Republicans felt increasingly burdened by the Southern question, and looked for a platform and candidate that could give the party fresh appeal. The Democrats, for their part, saw the election as an opportunity to clinch Southern "home rule," rid themselves of the stigma of treason and occupy the White House for the first time in 16 years.

Grant had become attached to the presidency, and if encouraged he might have tried for a third term. But Republican strategists saw him as a liability: People were tired of "Grantism" — even if they remained personally fond of the man who unwittingly had given his name to corruption.

In the spring of 1875, Pennsylvania Republicans adopted a resolution opposing the "election to the Presidency of any person for a third term." Grant had said little about his intentions until then, but he immediately announced that he would not accept renomination "unless it should come under such circumstances as to make it an imperative duty." Grant may have meant the statement as only a qualified withdrawal, but the Republicans accepted it as definitive.

By the time the Republicans held their national nominating convention in Cincinnati in June of 1876, the front-running candidate was James G. Blaine. An adroit and pragmatic politician from Maine who had been Speaker of the House for six years, Blaine appealed to the Republican leadership especially because of his reputation as a crusader against corruption. Responding to what they felt to be the mood of the country, the assembled Republicans adopted a reform program that had little to say about Reconstruction.

The black leader Frederick Douglass saw what was happening and raised some embarrassing questions: "What does it all amount to," he asked the delegates, "if the black man, after having been made free by the letter of your law, is to be subject to the slaveholder's shotgun?" The real question for the white delegates to ponder, Douglass said, was whether "you mean to make good to us the promises in your Constitution."

But the delegates' attention was elsewhere. When Blaine's record proved tarnished — he had been involved in a shady railroad deal — Liberal Republicans headed by Senator Schurz sought a compromise candidate. They found him in Rutherford Birchard Hayes — a former Union general and governor of Ohio who combined a good reform record with moderate Southern views. The liberals made him pledge to end Northern intervention in the South, then promised their support. He was nominated on the seventh ballot. Hayes's campaign stressed civil service reform and the right of Southerners to govern themselves. On civil rights he was purposely vague, saying only that "there can be no enduring peace if the constitutional rights of any portion of the people are permanently disregarded."

The Democrats nominated Governor Samuel J. Tilden of New York, a wealthy lawyer who had also made a name for himself as an anticrime crusader. While serving as chairman of the Democratic state committee, Tilden had fought New York's Tweed Ring, and had exposed the "Canal Ring" that for years had defrauded the state by submitting inflated repair bills involving the Erie Canal. Tilden was a cold but brilliant man whose ideology was fairly close to that of Hayes. Predictably, the Democratic platform stressed local self-government and national harmony, and attacked the failure and fraud of carpetbagger governments.

For a time, the campaign was relatively restrained. Then events in South Carolina — and the need for an issue — drove Hayes and the Republicans to take a harder line. South Carolina was in the midst of its own election campaign, with Massachusetts-born Governor Daniel H. Chamberlain running for reelection against the well-known planter and ex-Confederate General Wade Hampton.

The Yale-educated Chamberlain had given South Carolina its first honest administration in years, earning considerable Democratic support. But white supremacists rejected a carpetbag Republican and turned to Hampton as the man most capable of restoring home rule. Facing an uphill battle against a heavy pro-Chamberlain black vote, the Hampton Democrats determined on a campaign of brutality and intimidation. "It was generally believed," said South Carolina Senator Ben Tillman, "that nothing but bloodshed and a good deal of it could answer the purpose of redeeming the state."

The worst of the bloodshed occurred in the mostly black town of Hamburg, which lay across the Savannah River from the predominantly white city of Augusta, Georgia. Tension between the two populations flared into violence after a group of whites passing through Hamburg on July 4, 1876, found their way blocked by a black militia company that was drilling in celebration of the holiday. One of the whites declared angrily, "this is the rut I always travel and I don't intend to get out of it for no damned niggers." To avert trouble, the black company eventually parted to let the whites pass. But the matter did not end there.

A few days later, the militiamen were charged by the local magistrate with "obstructing the public highway." Hamburg by then was swarming with armed white men belonging to vigilante groups known as Sabre Clubs. When the blacks refused the magistrate's demand that they apologize and surrender their rifles, the whites set out to take the arms by force.

About 60 black militiamen retreated into the town's brick armory. After a spirited exchange of gunfire, the whites stormed and took the building. Prisoners were placed under guard while those who had fled were tracked down with bloodhounds. Five blacks identified as ring leaders were taken to a cornfield, were told to run and then were shot down while "attempting to escape."

The President condemned the Hamburg Massacre as "violence such as would hardly be accredited to savages, much less to a civilized and Christian people." But he took no action at first to correct the situation.

The most visible effect of such disorder on the 1876 presidential campaign was to heat up Republican oratory. "Every man that shot Union soldiers was a Democrat!" cried Robert G. Ingersoll of New York. "The man that assassinated Lincoln was a Democrat. Soldiers, every scar you have on your heroic bodies was given you by a Democrat." James Blaine took the stump for Hayes and urged all Union veterans to "vote as they shot."

# Celebrating a Century of Progress

Despite the troubles of Reconstruction, America in the 1870s was surging with optimism. Nowhere was this more evident than at the Grand Exposition held to commemorate the nation's Centennial in 1876. Ten million people paid 50 cents apiece to visit the 450-acre fairground in Philadelphia's Fairmount Park, where five spacious exhibition halls and a hundred smaller pavilions housed multinational displays of the latest art, fashion, produce and appliances.

"A tour through the halls and grounds," marveled one visitor, "was like a journey around the world." But the most popular exhibits were the huge industrial engines in Machinery Hall; more than anything else, these American-made dynamos exemplified the emergence of the United States as a world power.

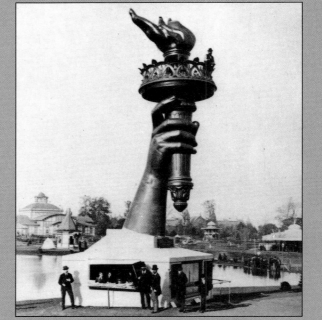

The upraised right arm and torch of sculptor Frédéric Auguste Bartholdi's colossal Statue of Liberty was erected on the grounds of the 1876 Centennial Exposition. Not until 1886 was the completed work dedicated in New York Harbor.

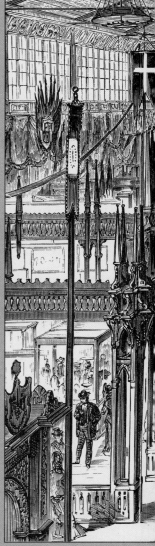

Visitors to the Centennial stroll among the international exhibits housed in the Exposition's main building. Six hundred yards long and covering 21 acres, the glass and steel structure was the largest in the United States.

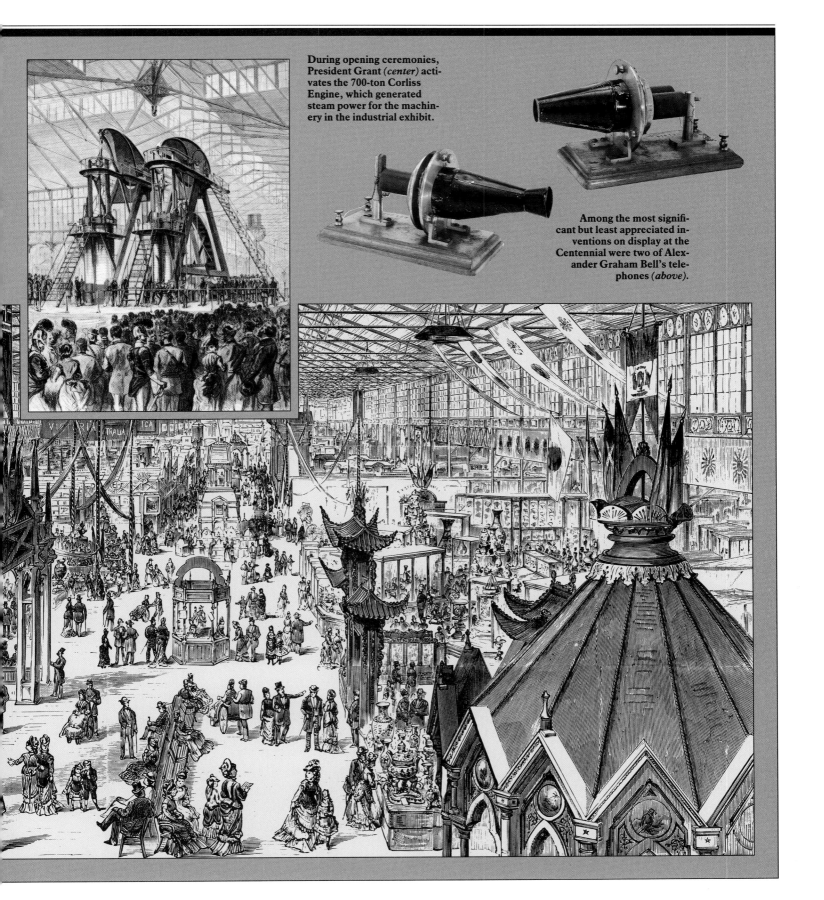

During opening ceremonies, President Grant (center) activates the 700-ton Corliss Engine, which generated steam power for the machinery in the industrial exhibit.

Among the most significant but least appreciated inventions on display at the Centennial were two of Alexander Graham Bell's telephones (above).

The usually moderate Hayes seemed to approve. "Our strong ground is the dread of a solid South, rebel rule, etc., etc.," he wrote to Blaine. "I hope you will make these topics prominent in your speeches. It leads people away from 'hard times,' which is our deadliest foe." For their part, Tilden and the Democrats accused Republicans of corruption, economic mismanagement and domination by the industrial interests.

On election night in November, leaders of both parties thought Tilden had won. He carried most of the South, as well as Connecticut, Indiana, New Jersey and New York. In Florida, Louisiana and South Carolina, both sides were claiming victory. Even without them, Tilden had 184 electoral votes, just one short of victory. Moreover, he was leading Hayes by an estimated quarter million popular votes. Republican National Chairman Zachariah Chandler went to bed sure that Tilden had been elected.

Early in the morning, Chandler was awakened at his hotel by New York *Times* editor John C. Reid and Republican National Committeeman William E. Chandler. They wanted his approval of a brazen scheme to capture the four disputed electoral votes of Florida, the eight disputed votes of Louisiana and the seven votes of South Carolina. With these 19 votes in the Republican column, Hayes would be the winner — by 185 electoral votes to 184.

Although the Republican chairmen in Louisiana and Florida were rumored to have already conceded to the Democrats, wires now went out telling them to hold their states at all costs. Zachariah Chandler audaciously announced that "Hayes has 185 electoral votes and is elected." The Republicans then set about making this claim a reality.

Both parties sent observers south to oversee the work of the election review boards, and accusations of fraud and intimidation were rampant. On both sides, wrote former Union General Lew Wallace to his wife, "nothing is so common as the resort to perjury. Money and intimidation can obtain the oath of white men as well as black: I do not know whom to believe."

The Republican-controlled boards in the three states dutifully looked over the returns, proclaimed Democratic fraud and announced a Republican sweep. Impassioned

When Rutherford B. Hayes, shown here flanked by his sons Webb (*left*) and Birchard, was belatedly declared winner of the 1876 election, the Republicans acted swiftly to preempt any Democratic effort to usurp the office. President Grant, whose term expired on March 4, 1877, had arranged a private swearing-in for Hayes on the evening before; the official inauguration ceremony proceeded as scheduled on March 5.

Democratic protests and cries of "Tilden or fight" were met by Republican evidence of massive stuffing of ballot boxes — far more votes were cast in South Carolina, for example, than there were registered voters. Rumors spread that militant Democrats were drilling under arms, and somebody fired a shot into the Hayes residence in Columbus. Amid talk of a new Civil War, President Grant strengthened the garrison in Washington. Tilden counseled his supporters against hasty action. "It will not do to fight," he told them — adding that another civil war "would end in the destruction of free government."

In this chaos, the Democratic House claimed the right to choose the President according to a constitutional provision empowering it to break a deadlock when there was no electoral majority for either candidate. The Republicans, knowing that this would mean Tilden's election, replied that the president of the Senate, a Republican, had the sole constitutional right to count disputed votes and declare a winner. The end of 1876 approached with no clear prospect of choosing a President before Grant's term expired on March 4. Disputes on the Senate and House floors reminded observers of the scenes in Congress on the eve of Secession.

At length Congress appointed a bipartisan commission to try to break the deadlock. The commission assigned the disputed electoral votes to Hayes, whereupon angry Democrats threatened a filibuster to obstruct the official counting of the electoral certificates by a joint session of Congress, and thus prevent Hayes's inauguration.

Out of this critical impasse emerged one of the most celebrated compromises in the annals of American politics. It had begun on December 12, 1876, with a letter to Hayes from Republican Congressman (and future President) James A. Garfield of Ohio. Despite all the noise the Democrats were making, said Garfield, he had the clear impression that "the Democratic businessmen are more anxious for quiet than for Tilden." Moreover, many Southern Democratic congressmen were "saying they have seen war enough." Garfield was sure that if the Southern Democrats became convinced the South would be kindly treated, a sizable number of them would throw their support to Hayes. The Republican candidate was delighted: "Your views are so nearly the same as mine," he replied, "that I need not say a word."

Hayes harbored a certain sympathy for the Southern ruling class. What he would like to see, he had suggested earlier to a college classmate from Texas, was an alliance of Northern and Southern conservatives against those who "make war on property." The men who ruled the postwar South, Hayes knew, shared many economic interests with the men who ruled the North and the Republican Party. Landed Southern families now shared political and economic power with a rising class of entrepreneurs involved in railroads, manufacturing and business enterprises of all kinds. For these men and for many others, observed Mississippi's Lucius Q. C. Lamar, it was more important "that the South should have self-government than that the President should be a Democrat."

The delicate task of bringing Democrats of Lamar's persuasion into the Hayes camp was undertaken by various mediators. The candidate himself kept quiet while his backers spread the word that he was a friend of the South who could be relied on to support home rule in Louisiana, Florida and South

Carolina, and favor government subsidies to aid in the South's development. This last was important to Southern business interests that had been lobbying for federal help in the construction of flood control projects in the Lower Mississippi valley, along with various canals, harbors, highways and railroads.

Included in the complex negotiations was an unwritten pledge of assistance to the Texas & Pacific Railroad. Chartered by Congress in 1871, the railroad had nearly gone bankrupt in the panic of 1873. Without a federal subsidy it could not possibly push on to the

Pacific coast as originally planned. Southern commitment to the line was fed by both greed and regional pride: It promised to make millions for investors by breaking the Northern monopoly and funneling traffic into the West by way of the South. Hayes's men let it be understood that the candidate was solidly behind completion of the line.

Although the negotiators tried to keep their activities quiet, Washington was soon alive with rumors that a deal was brewing. Deploring the apparent disloyalty of Southern Democrats, the pro-Tilden Cincinnati

# Misadventures in Egypt

Not all Civil War veterans were content to live out their lives as civilians, or at reduced rank in the Regular Army. Some three dozen former Union and Confederate officers found an exotic outlet for their military ambitions in the army of Ismail Pasha, Khedive of Egypt.

The charismatic Ismail had embarked on a program of modernization through which he hoped to gain autonomy for his impoverished country, which was a protectorate of Turkey. He hired Thaddeus Mott, an ex-colonel in the Union cavalry, to recruit fellow veterans as advisers for the undisciplined and poorly equipped Egyptian Army. Promising a yearly salary of $2,500 in gold, Mott

lured to Cairo a cadre of experienced American military men (*opposite*), among them six former generals.

The venture soon turned into a series of frustrations: General Charles P. Stone, the Khedive's chief of staff, found his efforts crippled by a corrupt bureaucracy, and General William W. Loring complained that the Egyptians lacked the "intellectual stamina" to develop an efficient officer corps. An embarrassing defeat at the hands of Abyssinian tribesmen confirmed their view, and by 1878 all but Stone had returned home. Most shared the opinion of Colonel Samuel H. Lockett, who called his time in Egypt "a miserable humbug — all show, all bunk, all make-believe."

The double-breasted frock coat and cork "solar helmet" above were worn by Colonel Samuel Lockett, a West Point graduate and former Confederate officer who spent two years in the Egyptian army.

"cheering continually." The balconies were crowded with ladies who waved their handkerchiefs and smiled on the troops below.

The steamer *Palace* waited at the levee. The cheers became "deafening," recalled the *Picayune* reporter, as the troops boarded and the ship edged away into the current. Trailing a long plume of smoke, the *Palace* picked up steam, swung gracefully about and headed down the Mississippi. The people of New Orleans stared after it until it dwindled and disappeared. The army's occupation of the South was to all intents over.

Reconstruction too had ended, and in many ways it had failed. When the last Republican governments fell, leaving a solidly Democratic South, the social structure of the region had changed little since 1860. The former landowners now shared their traditional leadership role with the new industrialists, to be sure, but power remained concentrated in the hands of a very small, white elite.

After being included briefly in the nation's first genuinely democratic governments, blacks now experienced disenfranchisement and exclusion from the political process. Economic inequities remained enormous in a region that lagged even further behind the North than it had before the War. Ironically, the Reconstruction years that were meant to bring social upheaval to the defeated Confederacy had left the infrastructure of the Old South fairly intact while changing the victorious North in ways few had foreseen.

Yet that was only part of the story. Beneath the surface, changes had been set in motion that would be felt in the South across future generations. The democratic franchise that blacks exercised during the Reconstruction years became a permanent part of their heritage, providing inspiration for the social change that occurred during the civil rights movement a century later. The 14th and 15th Amendments, which could have been adopted only in response to the pressures of Radical Reconstruction, furnished the legal framework for future assertion of civil and political rights. And although the South's black population was unmercifully

Only a federal soldier stands between a defenseless black man and vindictive Southern whites in this engraving from *Harper's Weekly*, which expressed Northern fears of the violence that would follow the removal of federal troops from the South.

Former President Grant and his wife Julia (*center*) prepare to visit a silver mine in Virginia City, Nevada, in 1879. Grant, like the rest of the country, longed to put the tumultuous years of Reconstruction behind him, and for more than two years after leaving office he and Julia traveled over much of the world. They finally settled in New York City, where Grant wrote his memoirs, completing them shortly before his death in 1885.

exploited by the share-cropping system, the notion of a free, competitive labor market took root as an ideal and an aspiration.

Beyond that, Reconstruction firmly established the principle of taxation for education, and of education — albeit segregated — regardless of race. And the carpetbag legislatures committed government to an array of social services in a region chronically in need of them. Perhaps most important, the Reconstruction era discredited forever the notion of force — or of secession — as a means of settling domestic controversy. However reluctantly they were brought to the conclusion, the people of the North and South were agreed at the end of Reconstruction that they were indissolubly one people.

In 1866, only a year after Appomattox, the women of Columbus, Mississippi, placed flowers on the graves of some federal soldiers who had died there in a Union hospital. It was the first recorded postwar tribute to the enemy dead. In time, such acts of reconciliation became almost routine in both the North and South. Memorial Day in particu-

lar became an occasion when Northern and Southern veterans honored the dead of both sides — everyone, in the words of the Boston *Daily Advertiser*, now "esteeming themselves Union men."

Beginning in the mid-1870s, veterans of the two sides held joint reunions, shared wartime memories and returned captured battle flags to the states whose regiments had lost them. In 1875, Brigadier General William Francis Bartlett, a much-wounded Union hero, attracted wide attention by declaring at ceremonies in Massachusetts that he was "as proud of the men who charged so bravely with Pickett's division on our lines at Gettysburg, as I am of the men who so bravely met and repulsed them there." By 1886, Henry W. Grady, the distinguished Georgia editor and spokesman for the postwar South, could say to a New York audience that he was glad an "omniscient God held the balance of battle in His Almighty hand, and that human slavery was swept forever from American soil — the American Union saved from the wreck of war."

# Twilight for the Blue and Gray

"The world will never see their like again," declared a spectator at a gathering of
Civil War veterans in 1903. "And as their ranks diminish, the reverence felt for
the survivors will increase." Indeed, for as long as they lived, the old soldiers, like the
gray-bearded ex-Federal in the photograph below, held an emotional grip on
successive generations of Americans.

In the years immediately following Appomattox, the 1.5 million Federal veterans were
hailed in the North as saviors of the Union; in the South, the 500,000 former
Confederates were venerated as martyrs of the Lost Cause. As the Civil War became
history over the years, these blood foes found themselves linked in what novelist
Stephen Crane called a "mysterious fraternity," and the men of both sides became patriotic symbols for all their countrymen.

Most veterans exulted in the reconciliation. "Our lives were mercifully spared," one
former Union officer told a group of former Confederates after the Spanish-
American War, "to see the sons of the old soldiers of the North stand shoulder
to shoulder with the sons of the old soldiers of the South." But for some, the wartime
passions would never dim. Seventy-three years after the end of hostilities, a few
90-year-old Federal veterans threatened to boycott the last reunion of Blue and Gray at
Gettysburg because the Confederate flag was to be displayed on that hallowed ground.

## Brotherhoods Born of Battle

As early as 1863, veterans in both the North and the South began banding together in fraternal organizations dedicated to preserving wartime friendships, caring for crippled comrades, honoring the dead and providing for their widows and orphans.

The largest Union organization was the Grand Army of the Republic. With posts all over the nation and a peak membership of 425,000, the GAR became a powerful lobby for Union veterans' benefits and was influential well into the 20th Century. Its smaller but regionally potent Southern counterpart was the United Confederate Veterans.

Members of the GAR post in Carlisle, Pennsylvania, some wearing badges made of brass melted down from a Confederate cannon, gather in front of their flag in about 1900. The veterans met regularly, said an observer, "to sing old war songs, tell old war stories and transact their business of charity."

GAR MEMBERSHIP BADGE

Former Union Generals (*left to right*) Lawrence P. Graham, Daniel E. Sickles and Eugene A. Carr tour Gettysburg in 1886. Sickles, who had lost a leg at Gettysburg, was a leader in the movement to turn the battlefield into a national shrine.

Southern Cross of Honor

Silas C. Buck of the United Confederate Veterans proudly displays the battle flag he carried at Mobile, Alabama, in 1865 as a 17-year-old color-bearer for the 10th Mississippi Cavalry. When Buck's unit surrendered, the youth hid the flag from his captors, then gave it to a Confederate officer for safekeeping.

The Old Guard of Richmond, a UCV affiliate, assembles at the Virginia Soldiers' Home in 1897 to raise funds for a monument honoring the legendary cavalry leader J.E.B. Stuart. Each member is wearing the uniform he had on when Lee surrendered at Appomattox in 1865.

## Valor Preserved in Stone

North and South, the veterans' organizations pressured state legislatures and solicited private funds to erect monuments honoring wartime deeds of valor. Soon almost every village had at least a stone or tablet honoring the men who had fought; memorial halls and heroic statues proliferated in cities and on the major battlefields. The intent behind the memorials was reflected in one old soldier's prayer at a dedication ceremony at Antietam: "I beseech Almighty God that this and all similar monuments may teach our children's children lofty lessons of American patriotism."

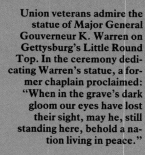

Ribbons such as the one below were given to members of the Duryeé Zouave Veterans Association, which led the nationwide funding drive for General Warren's Gettysburg memorial (*left*). The association's president called the journey to the dedication ceremonies "our pilgrimage."

Union veterans admire the statue of Major General Gouverneur K. Warren on Gettysburg's Little Round Top. In the ceremony dedicating Warren's statue, a former chaplain proclaimed: "When in the grave's dark gloom our eyes have lost their sight, may he, still standing here, behold a nation living in peace."

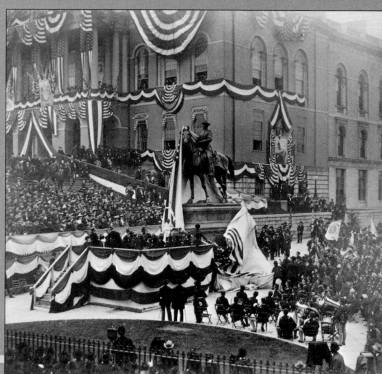

An equestrian statue of Major General Joseph Hooker, commissioned by the State of Massachusetts, is unveiled in Boston in 1903. Before the ceremony, Massachusetts veterans who had fought under Hooker 40 years earlier, marched through the city.

162

The souvenir ribbon shown here reads:

LAYING THE
CORNER STONE

LEE MONUMENT
RICHMOND, VA.
OCTOBER 27TH, 1887.

The souvenir ribbon above was sold at the 1887 cornerstone-laying of the Robert E. Lee monument in Richmond. The event saluted French sculptor Antonin Mercié for winning the competition to design the monument honoring Lee.

Southern veterans gather beneath the brooding statue of a Confederate private in Alexandria, Virginia, on the site where the young men of the city mustered in May 1861 before marching off to join Robert E. Lee. Inscribed on the pedestal are the names of Alexandria's 97 Confederate dead and Lee's tribute to them: "They died in the consciousness of duty faithfully performed."

Singing "Dixie," hundreds of children form a Confederate flag under the completed statue of General Lee at a 1907 reunion in Richmond. During the course of the four-day celebration, additional monuments were unveiled honoring Jefferson Davis and J.E.B. Stuart.

## A Holiday Honoring Those Who Fell

The custom of strewing flowers on the graves of dead soldiers, begun by Southern women, was formalized as Memorial Day in 1868 by ex-Union General John A. Logan, the Commander in Chief of the GAR. Logan ordered all GAR posts to organize parades to their local cemeteries, where they decorated the graves of fallen comrades. He selected May 30 as the date because so many flowers are then at their peak. Martial music, speeches and fireworks became part of the annual event — although many Southern states continued to celebrate Confederate memorial days on different dates.

Wearing their wartime uniforms, former members of the 165th New York Zouaves stride vigorously down a Brooklyn street during a 1903 Memorial Day parade. Forty years earlier, the ex-soldiers were part of the Union force besieging Port Hudson, Louisiana — the last Confederate bastion on the Mississippi River.

Led by a brass band, U.S. Army troops from nearby Fort Marcy parade through Santa Fe, New Mexico Territory, on May 30, 1880. The following year, the GAR adopted a resolution advocating that the holiday be officially designated "Memorial Day," not "Decoration Day" as some states called it.

A MEMORIAL DAY POSTCARD

A former Confederate cavalryman rides through a crowd of enthusiastic spectators during a reunion of Southern veterans in New Orleans in 1903.

## Asylum for Yesterday's Heroes

In 1865, Congress established asylums for Union veterans in Augusta, Maine; Dayton, Ohio; and Milwaukee, Wisconsin. But these homes soon were so overcrowded, complained a GAR official, that it was "impossible to get a needy soldier into them." So Northern states began to set up their own homes. State-supported and private institutions were the only recourse for ex-Confederates in need. "It is a comfort to the old veterans," a benefactor of the Maryland Confederate Home declared, "that a haven is provided to which they may retire and lose none of their self-respect."

The Cooper Shop Soldiers' Home in Philadelphia issued the handsomely illustrated receipt at left in exchange for a charitable contribution. Before the War ended, local philanthropists had chartered the home as a retreat for honorably discharged soldiers and sailors.

One-legged Union veterans play croquet on the lawn of the state capitol in Lansing, Michigan. A former soldier, explaining the GAR's campaign for additional veterans' hospitals, stated: "Empty sleeves, single legs, eyeless sockets and emaciated bodies point out the demand for organized work."

Two elderly veterans play checkers at the Confederate Soldiers' Home in Pewee Valley, Kentucky. "It affords me pleasure," a sponsor of the home claimed, "to know that comforts are being enjoyed by these blameless martyrs who have reached the evening of life."

Retired Confederates while away their time in the comfortable sitting room of the Kentucky Soldiers' Home in 1904. Many of these veterans asked to be buried at a local cemetery, where the son of a dead comrade had commissioned a granite monument in their honor.

## Reliving the Days of Glory

Reunions, hosted by a different city each year, attracted thousands of enthusiastic veterans. The GAR called its gatherings "encampments," and they were attended by Presidents and Cabinet members — testimony to the society's political clout.

The veterans also flocked to their old bat-tlefields and, in at least one instance, units that had fought each other exchanged vis-its. In 1883, survivors of the 28th New York, beaten 21 years earlier at Cedar Mountain by the 5th Virginia, invited their erstwhile foes to Niagara Falls; in return, the New Yorkers visited Virginia.

A bugler summons his comrades in this program for the 1889 Confeder-ate States Cavalry reunion in New Orleans. At the reunion banquet, the gray-haired troopers sang again such tunes as "Bonnie Blue Flag" and "Ain't I Glad to Get Out of the Wil-derness." Instead of dining on their wartime fare of corn bread and cof-fee, however, the veterans feasted on a seven-course dinner.

The badge at far right, souvenir of a Confederate reunion, is made from a palmetto frond and displays a Con-federate and a South Carolina flag. The badge at near right was worn by UCV members at an 1887 reunion in Macon, Georgia — the last one at-tended by Jefferson Davis.

Members of three Pennsylvania units, the 28th and 147th Infantry and Knap's Independent Battery E, Light Artillery, share a reunion at Harpers Ferry, West Virginia. The three out-fits had fought side by side at the Bat-tle of Gettysburg in 1863.

This souvenir program (*right*), paid for by a railroad that did a brisk business transporting veterans to reunions, features an idealized campfire scene. In practice, most of those attending "encampments" stayed in comfortable hotels.

In a rare display of comradery, black and white members of the Grand Army of the Republic visit Andersonville's Providence Spring, a fount of fresh water that opened mysteriously in 1864, saving the lives of dehydrated Union prisoners. Most units of the GAR were racially segregated.

State representatives to GAR national encampments wore badges such as the one at near right with a California bear. Members wore badges identifying their local posts (*far right*), which were named in honor of one who died in battle — here, an officer of the 6th New Jersey.

GRAND ARMY OF THE REPUBLIC

34TH ANNUAL ENCAMPMENT

IN THE CITY OF CHICAGO
AUGUST 26TH TO 30TH
1900

37TH NATIONAL ENCAMPMENT
SAN FRANCISCO 1903
GAR

TWENTY SIXTH NATIONAL ENCAMPMENT
AARON WILKES
POST 23
G.A.R.
TRENTON N.J.
1892

# A Healing of Old Wounds

From across the nation on July 1, 1913, fifty-seven thousand Union and Confederate veterans converged on Gettysburg, Pennsylvania, to commemorate the 50th anniversary of the greatest battle ever fought on American soil. For four days the men tramped about the battlefield, reliving youthful deeds and listening to patriotic speeches. "Once again does this field tremble under the tread of a mighty host — not now in fear, but in joy," exulted Secretary of War Lindley M. Garrison. "This meeting is the final demonstration that the last embers of former times have been

The cover of the 1938 reunion program features United States and Confederate flags with 13 stars, symbolizing the linkage of both North and South to the original 13 states of the Union. Entertainment for the event had a strikingly modern tone: a demonstration of tank warfare and a simulated air attack on Gettysburg by B-17 bombers.

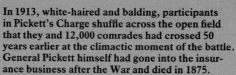

Each of the participants in the 1938 reunion received a personalized medal such as the one at right. Since most of the veterans were well past 90 years of age, and some were over 100, each was accompanied by a full-time attendant.

In 1913, white-haired and balding, participants in Pickett's Charge shuffle across the open field that they and 12,000 comrades had crossed 50 years earlier at the climactic moment of the battle. General Pickett himself had gone into the insurance business after the War and died in 1875.

stamped out. History knows no parallel."

The emotional peak of the celebration came on July 3, when 120 members of Major General George Pickett's division and 180 veterans of the Philadelphia Brigade reenacted Pickett's Charge. Separated by the same stone wall they had fought over in 1863, the men formed ranks 100 feet apart. At 3:15 p.m., the exact time the charge began, a color-bearer from each side ran forward and crossed battle flags. The Stars and Stripes was then raised above both banners and the former enemies advanced to the wall, clasped hands and embraced.

Twenty-five years later, 1,845 aged veterans returned to Gettysburg on the 75th anniversary of the battle to watch President Franklin D. Roosevelt dedicate the Eternal Light Peace Memorial. But soon they all would be gone — the last Union soldier died in 1956; the last Confederate in 1959.

Survivors of the Philadelphia Brigade (left) and Pickett's division join hands across the stone wall on Cemetery Ridge, where the Confederate charge was repulsed in 1863. "Your last memories of this field will overlay the earlier ones," a speaker told them. "It will no longer picture itself as a field of carnage and suffering, but a field of smiling faces and happy hearts."

# BIBLIOGRAPHY

## Books

Abbott, Martin, *The Freedmen's Bureau in South Carolina*. Chapel Hill: The University of North Carolina Press, 1967.

Adams, Henry, *The Education of Henry Adams*. Time Reading Program Special Edition. 2 vols. New York: Time Incorporated, 1964 (reprint).

Andrews, E. Benjamin, *The History of the Last Quarter-Century in the United States: 1870-1895*. Vol. 1. New York: Charles Scribner's Sons, 1896.

Bates, Gilbert H., *Sergeant Bates' March Carrying the Stars and Stripes Unfurled, from Vicksburg to Washington*. New York: B. W. Hitchcock, 1868.

Beale, Howard K., *The Critical Year: A Study of Andrew Johnson and Reconstruction*. New York: Frederick Ungar, 1958.

Beath, Robert B., *History of the Grand Army of the Republic*. New York: Bryan, Taylor, 1889.

Benedict, Michael Les, *The Fruits of Victory*. Ed. by Harold M. Hyman. Philadelphia: J. B. Lippincott, 1975.

Bentley, George R., *A History of the Freedmen's Bureau*. Philadelphia: University of Pennsylvania, 1955.

Blassingame, John W., *Black New Orleans: 1860-1880*. Chicago: The University of Chicago Press, 1973.

Botkin, B. A., ed., *Lay My Burden Down: A Folk History of Slavery*. Chicago: The University of Chicago Press, 1945.

Brock, W. R., *An American Crisis*. London: Macmillan, 1963.

Brown, Dee, *Bury My Heart at Wounded Knee*. New York: Holt, Rinehart & Winston, 1971.

Butler, Benj. F., *Butler's Book*. Boston: A. M. Thayler, 1892.

Callow, Alexander B., Jr., *The Tweed Ring*. New York: Oxford University Press, 1966.

Carleton, Mark T., *River Capital: An Illustrated History of Baton Rouge*. Northridge, Calif.: Windsor, 1981.

Carpenter, John A., *Sword and Olive Branch: Oliver Otis Howard*. Pittsburgh: University of Pittsburgh Press, 1964.

Carter, Hodding, *The Angry Scar: The Story of Reconstruction*. Garden City, N.Y.: Doubleday, 1959.

Catton, Bruce, *Grant Takes Command*. Boston: Little, Brown, 1969.

Chalmers, David M., *Hooded Americanism: The History of the Ku Klux Klan*. New York: Franklin Watts, 1981.

Coffman, Edward M., *The Old Army*. New York: Oxford University Press, 1986.

Cohen, Stan, *Hands across the Wall: The 50th and 75th Reunions of the Gettysburg Battle*. Charleston, W. Va.: Pictorial Histories, 1982.

Commager, Henry Steele, ed., *Documents of American History*. New York: Appleton-Century-Crofts, 1958.

Cooper-Hewitt Museum, *American Enterprise: Nineteenth-Century Patent Models*. Washington, D.C.: The Smithsonian Institution, 1984.

Craven, Avery, *Reconstruction*. New York: Holt, Rinehart and Winston, 1969.

Dawson, Joseph G., III, *Army Generals and Reconstruction*. Baton Rouge: Louisiana State University Press, 1982.

Dearing, Mary R., *Veterans in Politics: The Story of the G.A.R.* Baton Rouge: Louisiana State University Press, 1952.

Diamond, Sigmund, ed., *The Nation Transformed*. New York: George Braziller, 1963.

Dick, Everett, *The Sod-House Frontier*. Lincoln, Neb.: Johnsen, 1954.

Duberman, Martin B., *Charles Francis Adams*. Boston: Houghton Mifflin, 1961.

Foner, Eric, *Nothing but Freedom: Emancipation and Its Legacy*. Baton Rouge: Louisiana State University Press, 1983.

Franklin, John Hope, *Reconstruction: After the Civil War*. Chicago: The University of Chicago Press, 1961.

Freeman, Douglas Southall, *R. E. Lee: A Biography*. Vol. 4. New York: Charles Scribner's Sons, 1935.

Garraty, John A., *The Transformation of American Society, 1870-1890*. New York: Harper & Row, 1968.

Goldsborough, W. W., *The Maryland Line in the Confederate Army*. Gaithersburg, Md.: Butternut Press, 1983 (reprint).

Hackett, Frank Warren, *Reminiscences of the Geneva Tribunal of Arbitration 1872*. Boston: Houghton Mifflin, 1911.

Hesseltine, William B., and Hazel C. Wolf, *The Blue and the Gray on the Nile*. Chicago: The University of Chicago Press, 1961.

Horn, Stanley F., *Invisible Empire: The Story of the Ku Klux Klan 1866-1871*. Boston: Houghton Mifflin, 1939.

Hughes, Langston, and Milton Meltzer, *A Pictorial History of the Negro in America*. New York: Crown, 1956.

Jones, James Pickett, *John A. Logan: Stalwart Republican from Illinois*. Tallahassee: Florida State University, 1982.

Josephson, Matthew, *The Robber Barons*. New York: Harcourt Brace Jovanovich, 1962.

Katz, William Loren, *Eyewitness: The Negro in American History*. New York: Pitman, 1972.

Keller, Morton, *The Art and Politics of Thomas Nast*. New York: Oxford University Press, 1968.

Lewis, Lloyd, *Sherman: Fighting Prophet*. New York: Harcourt, Brace, 1932.

Litwack, Leon F., *Been in the Storm So Long: The Aftermath of Slavery*. New York: Alfred A. Knopf, 1979.

Logan, Rayford W., *Howard University: The First Hundred Years*. New York: New York University Press, 1969.

Long, E. B., with Barbara Long, *The Civil War Day by Day*. Garden City, N.Y.: Doubleday, 1971.

McElroy, Robert, *Jefferson Davis: The Unreal and the Real*. New York: Kraus Reprint, 1969.

McFeely, William S., *Grant: A Biography*. New York: W. W. Norton, 1981.

McKitrick, Eric L., *Andrew Johnson and Reconstruction*. Chicago: The University of Chicago Press, 1960.

McPherson, James M.:
*The Negro's Civil War*. New York: Pantheon Books, 1965.
*Ordeal by Fire: The Civil War and Reconstruction*. New York: Alfred A. Knopf, 1982.

Marszalek, John F., ed., *The Diary of Miss Emma Holmes*. Baton Rouge: Louisiana State University Press, 1979.

Meltzer, Milton, *In Their Own Words: A History of the American Negro*. New York: Thomas Y. Crowell, 1965.

Morgan, H. Wayne, ed., *The Gilded Age*. Syracuse, N.Y.: Syracuse University Press, 1963.

Morsberger, Robert E., and Katharine M. Morsberger, *Lew Wallace*. New York: McGraw-Hill, 1980.

Nevins, Allan, *The Emergence of Modern America: 1865-1878*. Vol. 8 of *A History of American Life*. Chicago: Quadrangle Books, 1955.

New York Monuments Commission for the Battlefields of Gettysburg and Chattanooga, *Final Report on the Battlefield of Gettysburg*. Vols. 2 and 3. Albany: J. B. Lyon, 1900.

Oberholtzer, Ellis Paxson, *A History of the United States since the Civil War*. Vols. 1, 2 and 3. New York: Macmillan, 1917-1926.

Paine, Albert Bigelow, *Th. Nast: His Period and His Pictures*. New York: Benjamin Blom, 1971.

Patrick, Rembert W., *The Reconstruction of the Nation*. New York: Oxford University Press, 1967.

Paxson, Frederic L., *History of the American Frontier: 1763-1893*. Boston: Houghton Mifflin, 1924.

Pennsylvania Commission, *Pennsylvania at Gettysburg*. Vol. 3. Harrisburg, Pa.: Pennsylvania Commission, 1914.

Pike, James S., *The Prostrate State: South Carolina under Negro Government*. New York: Loring & Mussey, 1935.

Randall, J. G., *The Civil War and Reconstruction*. Boston: D. C. Heath, 1937.

Reid, Whitelaw, *After the War: A Southern Tour*. Cincinnati: Moore, Wilstach & Baldwin, 1866.

Ripley, C. Peter, *Slaves and Freedmen in Civil War Louisiana*. Baton Rouge: Louisiana State University Press, 1976.

St. Hill, Thomas Nast, *Thomas Nast: Cartoons and Illustrations*. New York: Dover, 1974.

Sandburg, Carl, *Abraham Lincoln: The Prairie Years and the War Years*. New York: Harcourt, Brace & World, 1954.

Shenton, James P., *History of the United States from 1865 to the Present*. Garden City, N.Y.: Doubleday, 1964.

Smith, Page, *Trial by Fire: A People's History of the Civil War and Reconstruction*. Vol. 5. New York: McGraw-Hill, 1982.

Stampp, Kenneth M., *The Era of Reconstruction, 1865-1877*. New York: Vintage Books, 1965.

Stillwell, Leander, *The Story of a Common Soldier of Army Life in the Civil War: 1861-1865*. Collector's Library of the Civil War. Alexandria, Va.: Time-Life Books, 1981 (reprint).

Strode, Hudson, *Jefferson Davis, Tragic Hero*. New York: Harcourt, Brace & World, 1964.

Trefousse, Hans L., *Reconstruction*. New York: Van Nostrand Reinhold, 1971.

Trowbridge, J. T., *A Picture of the Desolated States; and the Work of Restoration*. Hartford, Conn.: L. Stebbins, 1888.

Utley, Robert M., *The Indian Frontier of the American West 1846-1890*. Albuquerque: University of New Mexico Press, 1984.

Warren, Robert Penn, *The Legacy of the Civil War*. New York: Random House, 1961.

Washington, Booker T., *Up from Slavery*. New York: Airmont Books, 1967.

Webb, Walter Prescott, *The Great Plains*. Boston: Ginn, 1959.

Wecter, Dixon, *When Johnny Comes Marching Home*. Cambridge, Mass.: Houghton Mifflin, 1944.

Williams, T. Harry, and the Editors of Time-Life Books, *The Union Restored*. Vol. 6 in The *LIFE* History of the United States. New York: Time-Life Books, 1974.

Wilson, Edmund, *Patriotic Gore: Studies in the Literature of the American Civil War*. New York: Oxford University Press, 1962.

Woodward, C. Vann, *Reunion and Reaction*. Boston: Little, Brown, 1966.

Wynes, Charles E., ed., *The Negro in the South since 1865*. University: University of Alabama Press, 1965.

## Other Sources

Brown, D. Alexander, "The Belknap Scandal." *American History Illustrated*, May 1969.

Donald, David, "Why They Impeached Andrew Johnson." *American Heritage*, December 1956.

"The Gray Parade." *Confederate Veteran*, July 1903.

Morsberger, Robert E., and Katharine M. Morsberger, "After Andersonville: The First War Crimes Trial." *Civil War Times Illustrated*, July 1974.

Peirce, Paul Skeels, "The Freedmen's Bureau." *Bulletin of the State University of Iowa*, March 1904.

"Reunion Retrospect." *Confederate Veteran*, June 1903.

"Unwritten History of Slavery." Social Science Source Documents, Fisk University, 1945.

## ACKNOWLEDGMENTS

The editors thank the following individuals and institutions for their valuable help in the preparation of this volume:

*Louisiana:* New Orleans — Pamela Arceneaux, The Historic New Orleans Collection; Pat Eymard, Confederate Museum; Pat McWhorter, Kitty Farley, Jan White, The Historical New Orleans Collection; Maud Lyon, Louisiana State Museum.

*Mississippi:* Biloxi — Keith Hardison, Beauvoir. Jackson — Mary Lohrenz, Mississippi State Historical Museum. Vicksburg — Gordon A. Cotton, Old Courthouse Museum.

*Ohio:* Fremont — Gilbert Gonzalez, Rutherford B. Hayes Presidential Center. Medina — JoAnn King, Medina County Historical Society.

*Pennsylvania:* Carlisle Barracks — Randy Hackenburg, Michael Winey, U.S. Army Military History Institute. Gettysburg — Larry Eckert, John Heiser, Robert Prosperi, Gettysburg National Military Park. Philadelphia — Russ A. Pritchard, The Civil War Library and Museum.

*South Carolina:* Columbia — John Martin, South Carolina Confederate Relic Room and Museum.

*Tennessee:* Greenville — Kent Cave, Andrew Johnson National Historical Site. Nashville — Beth M. Howse, Fisk University Library.

*Virginia:* Alexandria — Sam Story. Fort Belvoir — James Kochan, U.S. Army Engineers Museum. Richmond — David Hahn, Kay Lawson, Museum of the Confederacy; Greg Kimball, Valentine Museum; Linda Leazer, Virginia Historical Society. Lexington — Captain Robert C. Peniston, Lee Chapel, Washington & Lee University.

*Washington, D.C.:* Barbara Burger, Sharon Culley and staff, Still Pictures Branch, National Archives; Bernard Finn, Barbara Janssen, David Shayt, National Museum of American History, Smithsonian Institution; Eveline Nave, Photoduplication Service, Library of Congress; Mary E. Rephlo, Legislative Archives Division, National Archives.

*Wisconsin:* Madison — Richard H. Zeitlin, Grand Army of the Republic Hall Museum.

*Wyoming:* Cheyenne — John Langellier.

The index for this book was prepared by Roy Nanovic.

## Picture Credits

*Credits from left to right are separated by semicolons, from top to bottom by dashes.*

Cover: Library of Congress. 2, 3: Map by Peter McGinn. 8-13: Library of Congress. 14, 15: The New-York Historical Society. 17: National Park Service (NPS), Andrew Johnson National Historic Site, Greenville, Tennessee, photographed by Paul J. Pope. 19: Dupont Library, University of the South, Sewanee, Tennessee. 21: The Huntington Library, San Marino, California. 22: Dupont Library, University of the South, Sewanee, Tennessee; Beauvoir, Biloxi, Mississippi, photographed by Larry Cantrell — Library of Congress. 23: Confederate Memorial Hall, New Orleans, Louisiana, photographed by Jan White — drawing by Alfred R. Waud, Library of Congress. 24: The Valentine Museum, Richmond, Virginia — from *Frank Leslie's Illustrated Newspaper*, June 1, 1867 — State Historical Society of Wisconsin. 27: Ohio Historical Society, Columbus. 28: Painting by Edward Simmons, courtesy of the Massachusetts Art Commission, photographed by Mark Sexton. 30, 31: Library of Congress. 33: Painting by William L. Sheppard, Museum of the Confederacy, Richmond, Virginia, photographed by Katherine Wetzel. 35: Courtesy Frank & Marie-T. Wood Print Collections, Alexandria, Virginia. 37: Library of Congress; Louisiana Historical Association Collection, Manuscripts, Rare Books and University Archives, Tulane University Library. 38-41: Library of Congress. 44: Courtesy The New-York Historical Society. 45: From *Frank Leslie's Illustrated Newspaper*, February 2, 1867 — Arkansas History Commission, Little Rock, photographed by Bill Parsons. 46: Courtesy The New-York Historical Society. 47: Library of Congress — drawing by Alfred R. Waud, The Historic New Orleans Collection, Museum/Research Center, Acc. No. 1965.71. 48, 49: Courtesy William Gladstone Collection; Library of Congress; Rufus and S. Willard Saxton Papers, Yale University Library. 50, 51: Courtesy of Hampton University Archives; Moorland-Spingarn Research Center, Howard University. 53: Library of Congress. 55: NPS, Andrew Johnson National Historic Site, Greenville, Tennessee, copied by Paul J. Pope. 57: Library of Congress — Michael Miley Collection, Washington and Lee University Archives, Lexington, Virginia. 58, 59: The Valentine Museum, Richmond, Virginia; Museum of the Confederacy, Richmond, Virginia — painting by Adalbert Johann Volck, Valentine Museum, Richmond, Virginia. 60: Michael Miley Collection, Washington and Lee University Archives, Lexington, Virginia — Lee Chapel, Washington and Lee University, Lexington, Virginia, photographed by Katherine Wetzel. 62: Courtesy Herb Peck Jr. 65: The Children's Museum of Indianapolis, photographed by Dick Spahr. 66: Courtesy Frank & Marie-T. Wood Print Collections, Alexandria, Virginia. 68: Andrew Lytle Papers, LLMVC, Louisiana State University Libraries. 70: Library of Congress. 71: The Historic New Orleans Collection, Museum/Research Center, Acc. No. 1979.183. 73: Library of Congress. 74, 75: NPS, Andrew Johnson National Historic Site, Greenville, Tennessee, photographed by Paul J. Pope — National Archives SEN-40C-A2.RG 46(3); courtesy Frank & Marie-T. Wood Print Collections, Alexandria, Virginia. 77: Painting by Ole P. H. Balling, National Portrait Gallery, Smithsonian Institution. 79: Library of Congress. 80, 81: National Museum of American History, Smithsonian Institution, Washington, D.C., photographed by Dane A. Penland. 82-85: The Oakland Museum History Department. 86, 87: National Archives Neg. No. 59-HB-19, #45 American Image. 89: Courtesy the Kunhardt Collection. 90: Solomon D. Butcher Collection, Nebraska State Historical Society. 93: Library of Congress. 94, 95: Courtesy Larry J. West; National Archives Neg. No. 77-WA-11, #210 American Image — National Archives Neg. No. 106-WB-304; National Archives from *American Frontiers*, by Joel Snyder, Aperture Inc., Millerton, New York, 1981. 96, 97: Courtesy of the Edward E. Ayer Collection, The Newberry Library, Chicago. 99: Library of Congress. 100, 101: Inset, NPS, Custer Battlefield National Monument, copied by Brian Pohanka — National Archives Neg. No. 16-CN-2256, courtesy Fort Davis National Historic Site. 102, 103: National Archives Neg. No. 111-SC-85709 — National Archives Neg. No. 77-HQ-264-809; Stanley J. Morrow Collection, W. H. Over State Museum, Vermillion, South Dakota. 104, 105: Library of Congress; courtesy Robert Kotchian — Frederick Benteen Collection, Hargrett Rare Book and Manuscript Library, University of Georgia Libraries; National Archives American West #53. 107: Mississippi State Historical Museum, Mississippi Department of Archives and History, photographed by Gib Ford. 108: From *The History of the Last Quarter-Century in the United States 1870-1895*, by Elisha Benjamin Andrews, Charles Scribner's Sons, 1895. 109: Culver Pictures, Inc. 111: Library of Congress. 113: Painting by Thomas Le Clear, National Portrait Gallery, Smithsonian Institution. 114: Courtesy Frank & Marie-T. Wood Print Collections, Alexandria, Virginia. 115: General Research Division, The New York Public Library, Astor, Lennox and Tilden Foundations. 116: Library of Congress. 118: Tulane University Library, New Orleans. 119: Louisiana State Museum, photographed by Jan White. 121: Fisk University Library's Special Collections, Nashville, Tennessee. 122: Painting by Edgar Degas, Musée des Beaux Arts, Pau, photographed by Pierre Bérenger, Agence TOP, Paris. 126: Courtesy of The Mariners' Museum, Newport News, Virginia. 128, 129: National Archives Neg. No. 111-B-2947; engravings by Thomas Nast, courtesy Frank & Marie-T. Wood Print Collections, Alexandria, Virginia(2). 130-139: Engravings by Thomas Nast, courtesy Frank & Marie-T. Wood Print Collections, Alexandria, Virginia. 141: South Carolina Confederate Relic Room and Museum, photographed by Bud Shealy. 143: From *The History of the Last Quarter-Century in the United States 1870-1895*, by Elisha Benjamin Andrews, Charles Scribner's Sons, 1895. 144: Library of Congress(2); Brady-Handy Collection, Library of Congress, from *Mathew Brady: Historian with a Camera*, by James D. Horan © 1955, Bonanza Books, New York. 146, 147: Tennessee State Museum, Tennessee Historical Society Collection; Rutherford B. Hayes Presidential Center Neg. No. 369; Mississippi State Historical Museum, Mississippi Department of Archives and History, photographed by Gib Ford — Old Court House Museum, Vicksburg, Mississippi, photographed by Bob Pickett — Mississippi State Historical Museum, Mississippi Department of Archives and History, photographed by Gib Ford. 150, 151: Courtesy Frank & Marie-T. Wood Print Collections, Alexandria, Virginia. National Museum of American History, Smithsonian Institution, Washington, D.C., photographed by Dane A. Penland — The Historical Society of Pennsylvania; from *Frank Leslie's Historical Register of the United States Centennial Exposition, 1876.* 152: Library of Congress. 154, 155: U.S. Army Engineer Museum, Fort Belvoir, Virginia, photographed by Michael Latil(2); reprinted from *The Blue and the Gray on the Nile*, by William B. Hesseltine and Hazel C. Wolf, by permission of The University of Chicago Press, © 1961 by University of Chicago(3) — reprinted from *The Blue and the Gray on the Nile*, by William B. Hesseltine and Hazel C. Wolf, by permission of The University of Chicago Press, © 1961 by University of Chicago; U.S. Army Engineer Museum, Fort Belvoir, Virginia, copied by Michael Latil; The Valentine Museum, Richmond, Virginia; reprinted from *The Blue and the Gray on the Nile*, by William B. Hesseltine and Hazel C. Wolf, by permission of The University of Chicago Press, © 1961 by University of Chicago. 157: Courtesy Frank & Marie-T. Wood Print Collections, Alexandria, Virginia. 158, 159: Library of Congress. 160: U.S. Army Military History Institute (USAMHI), copied and photographed by A. Pierce Bounds. 161: Courtesy Kentucky Historical Society; courtesy Price Gibson and Associates, Hudson, Ohio, photographed by Jim Roetzel — Museum of the Confederacy, Richmond, Virginia. 162, 163: RG-25, Gettysburg Commission, Pennsylvania State Archives, Harrisburg — Massachusetts Commandery of the Military Order of the Loyal Legion of the United States and the U.S. Army Military History Institute (MASS-MOLLUS/

USAMHI), copied by A. Pierce Bounds; Gettysburg National Military Park, photographed by A. Pierce Bounds; Virginia Historical Society, Richmond, Virginia; Confederate Memorial Association, Washington, D.C. — from *Confederate Veteran*, July 1907, Vol. XV, No. 7, copied by Robert A. Grove. 164, 165: From *Album of the Second Battalion Duryee Zouaves, 165th Regiment New York Volunteer Infantry*, May 26, 1906, copied by Robert A. Grove — courtesy Roy Nuhn; USAMHI, copied by A. Pierce Bounds; original photograph at New Orleans Public Library, photograph courtesy The Historic New

Orleans Collection, Museum/Research Center, Acc. No. 1974. 25.21.17. 166, 167: USAMHI, photographed by A. Pierce Bounds; from *Confederate Veteran*, July 1908, Vol. XVI, No. 7, copied by Robert A. Grove — Michigan Department of State, State Archives, No. 11306; courtesy Kentucky Historical Society. 168, 169: The Historic New Orleans Collection, Museum/Research Center, Acc. No. 1951.49; Medina County Historical Society, photographed by Ron Linek; courtesy Price Gibson and Associates, Hudson, Ohio, photographed by Jim Roetzel; MASS-MOLLUS/USAMHI,

copied by A. Pierce Bounds; Michigan State University Archives and Historical Collections — MASS-MOLLUS/ USAMHI, copied by A. Pierce Bounds; Gettysburg National Military Park, photographed by A. Pierce Bounds; USAMHI, photographed by A. Pierce Bounds. 170: USAMHI, photographed by A. Pierce Bounds; Gettysburg National Military Park, photographed by A. Pierce Bounds — RG25, Gettysburg Commission, Pennsylvania State Archives, Harrisburg. 171: RG25, Gettysburg Commission, Pennsylvania State Archives, Harrisburg.

## INDEX

*Numerals in italics indicate an illustration of the subject mentioned.*

Pepper, George Whitefield, 78
Perry, "Major," 28
Petersburg, Virginia, 78
Philadelphia Brigade, *171*
Phillips, Wendell, 40, 52, 56, 156; letter by, *49*
Pickett, George, 170, 171
Pike, James Shepherd, 26, 117-118, 127
Pillsbury, Charles A., 83
Pinchback, Pinckney B. S., 69, 71
Pittsburgh, Pennsylvania, 83
Pool, John, 98
Pope, John, 61, 70
Pope Pius IX, gift to Jefferson Davis, *23*
Prescott, Arizona Territory, *105*
Promontory, Utah Territory, *84-85*
Pulaski, Tennessee, 36

**R**
Railroads: Credit Mobilier Affair, 109, 110; election campaigns, 54; expansion by, 83-86, 123, 154; and farmers, 89-90; parlor car, *86-87;* South, destruction in, 26; transcontinental routes, 78, 83, *84-85*, 154
Reconstruction: aftermath of, 157-158; black government during, 67-70; carpetbaggers, 63-64, 145; corruption in South, 66, 69, 117-119; election of 1876, 148-156; military districts in South, 61-63; Northern industrial interest in, 61; Panic of 1873, 127, 148; Republican plans for, 16-18, 30, 41, 52, 56, 112; State constitutional conventions, 65, 67-69; Union troops, withdrawal of, 156-157; voting rights in South, 63, 65, 156 ·
Reconstruction Acts, 56, 61, 63, 66, 70, 71, 75, 76
Red Shirts, uniform, *141*
Regiments. *See names of commanders, units, or under states*
Reid, John C., 152
Reid, Whitelaw, 29, 34, 123
Republican Party: carpetbaggers, 65; coalition in South, 66-67, *68*, 99; elephant symbol, 129, *139;* factions in, 16-17
Revels, Hiram Rhodes, 69, *70*
Richardson, Edmund, 124
Richardson, William, 112, 114, 116
Richmond, Virginia, 26, 61, *114*
*Rise and Fall of the Confederate Government,* 24
Robber barons, 86-88
Rockefeller, John Davison, 83, 86, 88
Roe, Frances, *104*
Roosevelt, Franklin D., 171
Rousseau, Lovell, 63

**S**
Sacramento, California, 84
St. Louis *Globe Democrat,* 115

Salisbury, North Carolina, 36
Sanborn, John D., 112-114
Sand Creek, massacre at, 93
Sante Fe, New Mexico, *164*
Savannah, Georgia, 59, 120
Scalawags, 63, 65-66
Schofield, John M., 61, 75
Schurz, Carl, 26, 110, 111, 127, 144, 149
Scranton, Pennsylvania, 79
Seward, William, 17, 31, 126
Seymour, Horatio, 61, 76
Sheppard, Ella, *121*
Sheridan, Philip H., 61, 63, 70, 72, *82, 130-131*, 144
Sherman, John, 77, 78, 97
Sherman, William T., *8-9*, 10, 76, *82, 96-97*, 111
Sholes, Christopher, 82
Shoshone Falls, Idaho Territory, *94*
Sickles, Daniel E., 61, 63, 70, *160*
Simpson, Matthew, 75
Sioux, 92, 96, 102, 103
Sons of Midnight, 36
South: convict leasing, 124; Democratic control, 148, 156; devastation in, 25-26; economic weakness of, 123; education, 120-123, 158; military districts and garrisons, map 2-3, 61-62, 63, 156-157; North, feeling against, 16, 18, 28; racial relations, 28, 64; secret organizations, 36, 76, 97-99, 120, 141, 142, *146-147*, 150; sharecropping, *42-44*, 123-124
South Carolina: corruption in, 66, 117-119; cotton plantation, *44;* devastation in, 26; education in, 29; land redistribution in, 120; readmission to Union, 69; violence in, 98, 99, 149-150
*Southern Cultivator,* 28
Southern Homestead Act of 1866, 36
Southern Pacific Railroad, 86
Sparta, Louisiana, 140
Springfield *Republican,* 85
Standard Oil Company, 83, 108
Stanford, Leland, 86
Stanton, Edwin M., 8, 17-18, 22, 32, 56, 70, 72-73
Statue of Liberty, torch, *150*
Stephens, Alexander H., 34, 145
Stevens, Thaddeus, 2, 33, 40, *41*, 72, *73*
Stillwell, Leander, 20-25
Stone, Charles, 154, *155*
Strong, George Templeton, 40, 52, 110, 125
Stuart, J.E.B., 161, 163
Sumner, Charles, 2, 33, 40, 106, 110, *134*
Supreme Court, 39, 40
Swank, James, 125
Swayne, Wager, 70
Swift, Gustavus F., 83, 86

**T**
Taylor, Bayard, 77
Taylor, Richard, 19
Taylor, Walter H., 57
Tennessee: anti-Klan laws in, 97; corruption in, 119; loyalist government in, 30, 32; readmitted to Union, 54; Union settlements in, 64
Tenure of Office Act, 56, 70, 72, 73
Texas, readmitted to Union, 69
Texas & Pacific Railroad, 154
Thomas, Lorenzo, 72
Tilden, Samuel J., 149, 152, 153, 155, 156
Tillman, Ben, 149
Titusville, Pennsylvania, 83
Towne, Laura M., 120, 123
Trowbridge, John Townsend, 16, 26
True, B. H., 64
Trumbull, Lyman, 39, 40
Turner, Henry, 36
Tweed, William Marcy (Boss), 109-110, 129, 149; Nast cartoon, *132-133*
Twitchell, Marshall Harvey, 140-142

**U**
Union Army: black soldiers, 47, *100-101;* casualties, 25; commanding generals, 77; discipline, *105;* Grand Review, *8-15;* Indian fighting and frontier garrisons, 93, *100-105;* military garrisons in South, 28, 61, *62*, 63; prison camp survivors, 37; returning veterans of, 20-25, 34, 78; supply wagons, *27, 102;* troop strength, 25, 28, 61, 143; veteran organizations and reunions, *159-171;* Veteran Reserve Corps, *8-9*
Union League, 67
Union Pacific Railroad, 83, *84-85*, 109
Union Party, 16
Union Trust Company, 125
Unions, development of, 89
United Confederate Veterans, 160, *161;* badge, *161*
United States Patent Office, 81
United States Regular Army: 7th Cavalry Regiment, 92, 93, 96, *101, 104-105;* 9th Cavalry Regiment, *100-101;* 3rd Infantry Regiment, 143, 156-157
United States Sanitary Commission, 78

**V**
Vallandigham, Clement, 110
Vanderbilt, Cornelius, 86, 106
Vermont troops, 4th Infantry Regiment, 140
Veteran Reserve Corps, *8-9*
Veterans: effect of war on, 25; reunions and organizations, 158, *159-171*
Vicksburg, Mississippi, 115, 145

Virginia: corruption in, 119; loyalist government in, 30, 32; readmission to Union, 69
Virginia City, Nevada, 158
Virginia troops, 5th Infantry Regiment, 168

**W**
Wade, Benjamin F., 16, 30
Wade-Davis Bill, 30
Walker, Francis A., 97
Wallace, Lew, 152
Warmoth, Henry Clay, 117
Warren, Gouverneur K., 162
Washington, Booker T., 48, *50*
Washington, D.C., 51; Capitol, *12*
Washington Arsenal, 38
Washington College, *58-59, 60*
Watterson, Henry, 112
Welles, Gideon, *8-9*, 17, 20, 31, 41, *55*, 110
Wells, David A., 88
West: cattle drives, 91-92; government survey expeditions, 94-95; mining in, 92; opening of, 77, 83-85, 90-91; railroads, 78, 83, *84-85*, 91; settlement by veterans, 25, 78, 91, 93; sod houses and homesteaders, *90;* Union supplies for, 27
West Virginia, racial violence in, 120
Wheeler, George, 94
Whiskey Ring, 115-116
White, George L., 121
White League, 142-144
White Liners, 145, 147
White Sulphur Springs, West Virginia, Confederate dignitaries at, *58*
Wilder, John T., 64
Wilder's Lightning Brigade, 64
Willey, Waitman T., 75
Wirz, Henry, *37-39*
Wisconsin troops, 2nd Infantry Regiment, 64
Wormley House Conference, 155-156

**Y**
Yazoo City, Mississippi, 64
Youngstown, Ohio, 79

**Z**
Zanesville, Ohio, 27
Zouave units, *14-15*, 162, *164*